Get the most from this

Everyone has to decide his or her own revision strategy, but it is essential to review your work, learn it and test your understanding. These Revision Notes will help you to do that in a planned way, topic by topic. Use this book as the cornerstone of your revision and don't hesitate to write in it — personalise your notes and check your progress by ticking off each section as you revise.

Tick to track your progress

Use the revision planner on pages 4 and 5 to plan your revision, topic by topic. Tick each box when you have:

- revised and understood a topic
- tested yourself
- practised the exam questions and gone online to check your answers and complete the quick quizzes

You can also keep track of your revision by ticking off each topic heading in the book. You may find it helpful to add your own notes as you work through each topic.

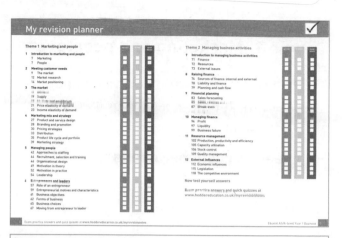

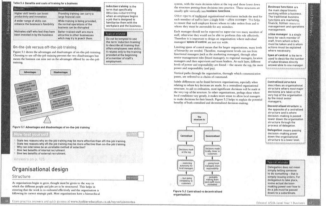

Features to help you succeed

Exam tips

Expert tips are given throughout the book to help you polish your exam technique in order to maximise your chances in the exam.

Typical mistakes

The author identifies the typical mistakes candidates make and explains how you can avoid them.

Now test yourself

These short, knowledge-based questions provide the first step in testing your learning. Answers are at the back of the book.

Definitions and key words

Clear, concise definitions of essential key terms are provided where they first appear.

Key words from the specification are highlighted in colour throughout the book.

Revision activities

These activities will help you to understand each topic in an interactive way.

Exam practice

Practice exam questions are provided for each topic. Use them to consolidate your revision and practise your exam skills.

Summaries

The summaries provide a quick-check bullet list for each topic.

Online

Go online to check your answers to the exam questions and try out the extra quick quizzes at **www.hoddereducation.co.uk/myrevisionnotes**

My revision planner

Theme 2 Managing business activities

REVISED   TESTED   EXAM READY

Now test yourself answers

Exam practice answers and quick quizzes at www.hoddereducation.co.uk/myrevisionnotes

Countdown to my exams

1 Introduction to marketing and people

Marketing

Marketing is the term used to describe the range of activities that businesses undertake to try to create a demand among consumers for their products or services. Marketing managers must ensure that they understand what is happening in the markets they sell to and how and why consumers behave the way in which they do. In order to gain this understanding, marketing departments carry out market research aimed at developing a genuine understanding of consumer behaviour. This allows them to make better decisions on how to entice consumers to decide to buy the products and services. In a modern marketing department, much of this research is gathered in real time from social media and minutely detailed analyses of sales data.

A summary of the work done by marketing departments can be seen in Table 1.1.

Table 1.1 Work done by marketing departments

Understanding markets	Making marketing decisions
Market research	Designing products and services
Analysing factors affecting demand in a market	Deciding on a price
Deciding which markets to sell to	Deciding where to distribute
Spotting changes within markets	Communicating with customers
Understanding consumer behaviour within markets	

People

Businesses need many different resources to enable them to meet their objectives. Physical resources such as buildings and equipment, as well as financial resources, must be well managed. Research shows that in the long run human resources are the most important. This is why so much time and attention is given to ensuring that businesses get as much from their people as possible.

Human resources departments are likely to take charge of the following activities:
- recruitment of new staff
- selection of applicants for jobs/promotions
- training new and existing staff
- designing and administering payment systems
- planning future workforce needs.

In smaller firms, without a specialist HR department, the boss will need to handle all these tasks, and others relating to the people who work for the business. Some larger businesses will also expect departmental managers and supervisors to take responsibility for other people-related tasks including:
- working out shift rotas
- coaching staff

- providing on-the-job training
- motivating staff on a day-to-day basis
- delegating authority.

A business can secure an advantage over its rivals through expert use of marketing and people in many ways. A selection of these is shown in Figure 1.1.

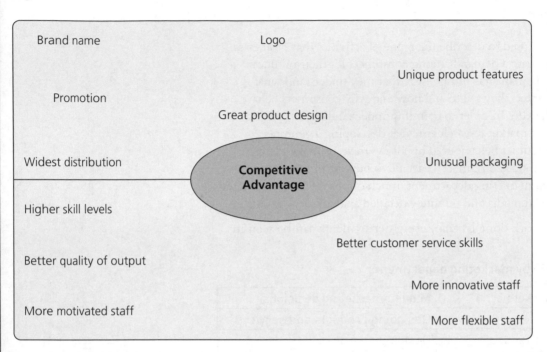

Brand name   Logo

Unique product features

Promotion

Great product design

Widest distribution   **Competitive Advantage**   Unusual packaging

Higher skill levels

Better customer service skills

Better quality of output

More innovative staff

More motivated staff

More flexible staff

Figure 1.1 Different ways in which businesses have advantages over their rivals

Now test yourself

TESTED

1 Briefly explain what makes the following successful products or services stand out from their rivals:
   (a) Apple's iPhone
   (b) Heinz Tomato Ketchup
   (c) John Lewis department stores
   (d) Cadbury's chocolate

Answers on p. 121

Summary

- Marketing is the business function whose role is to create a demand for a firm's products or services.
- The people in a business are a critical resource that needs to be used effectively.
- Marketing and people can both provide a competitive advantage.

2 Meeting customer needs

The market

A market exists where buyers and sellers meet in order to exchange goods or services. Though some markets can be identified as having a physical location, markets are best thought of as any occasion where a buyer and seller can interact and can therefore be online, by post or in a shopping centre or trade fair.

Mass markets and niche markets

REVISED

Some businesses will produce products and services aimed at satisfying the needs of a whole market, rather than any specific section of the market. Attempting to sell to the whole market is called mass marketing. Other businesses select a **segment** of the market and sell products specifically to suit the needs of consumers in that segment. This process is called **niche** marketing.

> A **market segment** is a subsection of a larger market in which consumers share similar needs and wants.
>
> A **niche market** is a small segment of a larger market.

Table 2.1 Benefits of different marketing strategies

Benefits of mass marketing	Benefits of niche marketing
Huge potential number of customers	Meeting consumer needs more precisely allows higher prices to be charged
Higher production levels allow economies of scale – lower production costs	Higher profit margins
Can use mass media advertising	Easier to enter for firms with limited financial resources

There are notable differences between mass and niche markets as shown in Table 2.2.

Table 2.2 Differences between mass and niche markets

	Mass market	Niche market
Characteristics	Generic products which are broadly similar in form and function	Specialist products and services are required. Changes in consumer preferences can be rapid and devastating to the market
Market size and share	Huge markets in which large firms can operate successfully even though their market share may be low, e.g. Ferrero's 5% share of the UK chocolate market	Smaller markets mean successful firms may achieve far higher shares of their niche than mass market firms
Brands	Huge brands can develop with the name/logo representing a key point of differentiation	Differentiation is more likely to be achieved through product features and functions

Dynamic markets

REVISED

No business can afford to stand still because markets are dynamic, they tend to change over time. There are four major issues to consider.

Online retailing

Continued growth in online retailing has varied between different markets, with clothing growing tremendously but growth in online sales of books slowing to a virtual halt. This unpredictability of growth adds to the unpredictability of dynamism in online retailing. What history has shown us is that retailers who fail to switch to online retailing can fail completely as online rivals steal sales. Above all, it is vital to ensure that your product or service is available to buy wherever consumers want to buy it. In some cases it is vital to have an online presence, or if consumers want to buy online and collect from their local store, a click-and-collect service is needed.

How markets change

Markets change as a result of major external influences, as summarised by the **PESTLE** acronym.

PESTLE highlights the major sources of external changes faced by businesses: Political, Economic, Social, Technological, Legal and Environmental.

Examples of market changes include the following:
- Political: In 2016 the government's new 'Living Wage' was brought in, pushing the legal minimum (for over-25s) from £6.70 to £7.20 an hour; this was great for low-paid employees, but tough on employers in low-wage industries such as care homes.
- Economic: The economic recession of 2008–09 led to major changes in UK grocery retailing, as price-conscious shoppers opted for Aldi and Lidl.
- Social: An increased desire for convenience has driven the rise in online retailing.
- Technological: 'Apps' did not exist ten years ago, prior to the advent of the smartphone; by 2016 they were capable of turning century-old markets on their head, as with taxis and the arrival of Uber.
- Legal: Growth in the market for e-cigarettes is being affected by the introduction of new laws relating to who can buy, how they can be advertised and where they can be consumed.
- Environmental: The car industry is facing major changes in order to try to minimise the damaging impact of exhaust fumes on the environment.

Innovation and market growth

A major cause of change within markets is innovation. With competing firms continually trying to develop new products and services that offer features that no rivals offer, consumer loyalties can change dramatically. Once one innovation has been successful, other companies may be forced to try to adapt their offerings in order to keep pace with rivals.

Furthermore, many companies will try to come up with their own innovations in order to try to benefit from leading change in the market.

Adapting to change

Market research and an understanding of general trends in the market are vital to successfully adapting to change. Identifying subtle changes in what consumers are looking for in their products allows businesses to adapt their products to better suit these needs. Whether it be removing sugar from food products or adding features to mobile phone handsets, changing earlier than rivals offers a major source of competitive advantage.

> **Typical mistake**
>
> Too often exam answers imply that adapting to change is a simple process for a business. These responses fail to show an appreciation of the impact on all four business functions: marketing, people, finance and operations. Required changes may include production methods, finding new suppliers, redeploying workers and adopting new advertising and distribution methods.

How competition affects the market `REVISED`

Competition is the feature of business that most stimulates change and development. This is especially clear in the battle between Apple and Samsung in the smartphone market. Neither can sit back for a moment. That was clear when the market was disappointed by Apple's iPhone 5, leading to significant gains for Samsung. It took a huge development effort for Apple to regain its supremacy with the iPhone 6.

Increased levels of competition create various pressures for businesses:
- The need to drive down costs.
- The need to maintain competitive prices.
- The need to develop innovative products and services.
- The need to maintain high quality of products and services.

The difference between risk and uncertainty `REVISED`

Operating a business in any market involves facing up to risk and coping with uncertainties. The key difference lies in the predictability of events occurring. A risk is quantifiable, so if statistics show that only 1 in 20 new consumer goods succeed, the risk involved in launching a new product can be identified and quantified. The factors causing the risk are the uncertainties – those factors that cause a lack of certainty in future events – such as reactions of rivals, reactions of consumers, reactions of retailers and such unexpected events as currency movements and economic downturns.

> **Typical mistake**
>
> Too many answers use the terms 'risk' and 'uncertainty' interchangeably – they are not the same thing.

Now test yourself `TESTED`

1 State two benefits of mass marketing.
2 State two benefits of niche marketing.
3 What are the six major external forces that lead to change in markets?
4 State three benefits experienced by consumers as a result of increased competition in a market.
5 What marketing activity tends to be the key to successfully adapting to change in markets?

Answers on p. 121

Market research

Product and market orientation

REVISED

Product orientation is an approach to making decisions that considers internal factors before worrying about changes in the market. This means that product-orientated businesses can focus on their own key strengths and this can lead to revolutionary new ideas that consumers would never have dreamed of. However, the danger is that the business fails to adapt its products in line with what consumers are looking for, which could lead to huge problems.

The opposite approach – market orientation – is more likely to lead to marketing success since it places consumers' views and behaviours at the heart of decision-making within the business.

Primary and secondary research

REVISED

Market research can use either secondary data or primary data, with **primary research** being new research carried out for the first time, and **secondary research** being research that uses data that had already been gathered for some other purpose.

The data gathered may be **quantitative** or **qualitative**. Quantitative data contains factual, often numerate data that is intended to be statistically representative of the whole market. Qualitative data contains opinion and is unlikely to have been gathered on a large enough scale to give statistically reliable data. It is designed to give insight into why customers behave the way they do.

Primary research is new research conducted for a particular purpose.

Secondary research uses pre-existing data that has been gathered for another purpose.

Typical mistake

Primary research does not have to be carried out by individual businesses. They can hire a market research company to do the research for them. If it is new research, it is still primary.

Table 2.3 Advantages and disadvantages of primary and secondary research

	Secondary research	Primary research
Advantages	• Often free • Provides a good market overview • Usually based on large-scale, reliably produced research	• Addresses the specific issues you are interested in • Data is up to date • Can help to understand customer psychology
Disadvantages	• Information may be out of date • Not tailored to suit your particular needs • Can be expensive to buy published research reports on markets	• Expensive, costing thousands of pounds to do properly • Risk of bias from questionnaire and interviewer • May need to compare with other information to understand the meaning of findings

Quantitative research is research conducted on a large-enough scale to provide statistically reliable data, usually aimed at discovering factual information about how customers behave.

Qualitative research is unlikely to be carried out on a large-enough scale to give statistically valid data, but is instead aimed at providing insights as to why customers behave the way they do.

Exam tip

Generally most firms will use a combination of secondary and primary research, with secondary often conducted first to help design the primary research needed without incurring the high cost of primary research first.

Table 2.4 Different primary and secondary research methods

Secondary research methods	Primary research methods
The internet	Surveys
Trade press	Retailer research
Government statistics	Observation
Past internal sales figures	Group or individual discussions

Limitations to market research

REVISED

If all market research provided accurate and reliable data, then all businesses would succeed. There are two major reasons why market research data may be unreliable:

- Sample size too small: This means that there is more chance that respondents who do not reflect the overall views of the market are over-represented in the sample.
- Sample bias: The way that respondents are selected may over-represent certain types of people whose views may skew the overall findings away from the views of the total population being researched.

> **Exam tip**
>
> Using the wrong research method may not be the major mistake made by a business whose research seems to let them down. Analysing and then interpreting market research data correctly is the most common problem within the marketing process. The best marketing decision-makers use surveys to provide insights – but they still take the key decisions based as much on experience and intuition as on research.

Use of ICT to support market research

REVISED

There are three main ways in which ICT can support market research:

- Company websites can gather data on visitors to the website which can provide some information about online shoppers' or browsers' interests.
- Social media can also offer information on consumer attitudes to a product or service, and even allow for an element of relationship building between the business and consumers.
- Database technology, which has advanced so far in recent years, allows vast quantities of data relating to consumers to be trawled in order to identify patterns that can help to explain how consumers actually behave, with much of this data being generated by loyalty cards.

> **Typical mistake**
>
> Despite their name, a major purpose of loyalty schemes is to gather information on customers' buying habits.

Market segmentation

REVISED

One main function of market research is to help to decide on useful ways to **segment markets**. Splitting markets up helps to target specific groups of consumers who share similar needs and wants, enabling a firm to meet these more closely. Market research can unearth insights that allow firms to identify segments that they can fulfil profitably.

Benefits of segmenting a market include:

- Products and services can be designed to suit specific customers.
- Meeting customers' needs precisely allows a higher price to be charged.
- Promotional activity is easier to target.

> **Market segmentation** means discovering useful ways to split up a market into different groups of consumers who share similar characteristics and needs.

6 What type of research is aimed at finding out about customer attitudes in the hope of gaining insights into consumer behaviour?
7 What type of research uses data that has already been gathered for another purpose?
8 What type of research gathers brand new data?
9 What type of research is aimed at delivering statistically reliable information?
10 Is a product-orientated or market-orientated business more likely to come up with brand new, revolutionary product ideas?
11 State two reasons why market research may give misleading results.
12 List three ways that ICT can help with market research.
13 State three benefits of segmenting a market.

Answers on p. 121

Market positioning

Decisions over fine tuning the product being sold must follow earlier, strategic decisions about what products to sell to which markets. This fine tuning is the process of **market positioning**.

> **Market positioning** means deciding exactly what image you are trying to create for your product relative to its rivals.

Market mapping   REVISED

The two key judgements required in successful market mapping are:
● choosing the right variables to place on each axis
● placing rival brands in the right place on the map, truly reflecting consumer perceptions of those brands (see Figure 2.1).

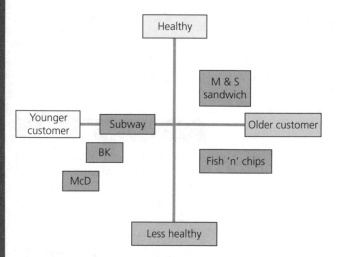

Figure 2.1 Market map of the UK fast food industry

With a market map produced, a business can identify the gaps in the market more easily. Following this is a check to ensure that the gap can be filled profitably. For example, drawing a map of the UK car market can identify a gap for a truly luxurious sports car selling for £10,000. Of course, the reason why this gap exists is that no firm is capable of making the product at a cost that will let them make a profit at a price of £10,000.

With a gap identified, the firm must then decide how to use the marketing tools at its disposal. Managers will want to create an image that matches the product to the gap that has been identified.

Competitive advantage

REVISED

Products without any competitive advantage over their rivals have been proven time and again to have no long-term future. The two major generic routes to finding a competitive advantage are to:

- be the lowest cost producer, e.g. Ryanair in the European airline market
- find a sustainable point of differentiation, e.g. KFC in the market for fast food.

Producing your product more efficiently and thus more cheaply than any rivals will ultimately allow a business to sell at a lower price than any other firm, yet still make a profit. Generally, in any given market there is space for one firm to fulfil this role of lowest-cost producer.

The key to competitive advantage is that it should be sustainable in the long term. A really strong brand name and image can achieve this, but only if the whole business focuses on providing the products and services that match or even enhance the brand.

Product differentiation

REVISED

Standing out from rivals can be achieved through actual, tangible differences between products or through manipulating consumer perceptions of your product – a kind of psychological differentiation. Possibilities are shown in Table 2.5.

Table 2.5 Tangible differences between products

Actual product differentiation	Perceived product differentiation
Design	Branding
Different functions	Advertising
Taste	Sponsorship
Performance	Celebrity endorsement

Product differentiation means attempting to make your product seem different, in the minds of consumers, to any other rival in the market.

The purposes of **product differentiation** are:

- insulating the product from the actions of competitors
- allowing prices to be increased without a major fall in demand or sales.

As we will see later, in Chapter 3, differentiation is the key to reducing a product's price elasticity.

Typical mistake

Be careful not to over-use the term 'unique selling point'. Many product features can differentiate a product without being actually unique.

Adding value

REVISED

Product differentiation generally helps to add value to products and services. The ability to push prices higher without increasing the costs of producing a product will naturally add value. Once more, **added value** may come about through tangible, engineering methods, such as creating a great design or finding a way to produce in a far cheaper manner, or it may be added through perception, generally through promotional methods such as advertising and branding. L'Oréal's slogan 'Because I'm worth it' is the company's clever way of persuading customers that paying a higher price for L'Oréal products is 'worth it', i.e. it adds value.

Added value is the difference between the cost of bought-in goods and services and the selling price of a product.

Now test yourself

14 What is market mapping designed to reveal?
15 What are the two main routes to competitive advantage?
16 Explain the effects that the arrival of Aldi and Lidl have had on Tesco in the UK grocery market.
17 Explain the main sources of competitive advantage for each of the following:
   (a) iPhone   (b) Yorkie   (c) Nando's
18 How can being the most efficient producer of a product create long-term success?
19 What are the two main benefits of successful product differentiation?
20 How can advertising add value to a product?

Answers on p. 121

Exam practice

The market for toys in the UK is highly seasonal. It is a market that has a strong record of innovation, especially in the development of electronic toys that use the latest audio-visual technology, and can often throw up surprise success stories. Over the past three years the market has grown as the UK's economy has recovered. As well as new toy products, some old products are also making a return. In the niche market of sports games, a Spanish company Netcam has relaunched Subbuteo table football in the UK. It decided to go ahead after studying the results of some quantitative research among boys. The game, which was first launched in the 1950s, had been withdrawn from the market in 2007. With the game beginning to appear in major toy retailers such as Argos and John Lewis, the relaunch seems to be proving a modest success. Nevertheless, many commentators have suggested that the company's failure to launch an e-commerce site through which Subbuteo products can be bought directly may be harming sales growth.

Questions

1 What is meant by quantitative research?   (2)
2 What is meant by niche market?   (2)
3 Explain how the use of a familiar brand name can help Netcam relaunch Subbuteo products.   (4)
4 Assess the major influences on the market size of the toy market examined in the item.   (10)

Answers and quick quiz 2 online

Summary

- Mass marketing and niche marketing are alternative approaches to marketing that both offer benefits and drawbacks.
- Markets are dynamic. They change, raising the following issues for businesses: how markets change, the rise of online markets, innovation in markets and adapting to change in markets.
- Competition is a key driving force behind features within markets such as prices, quality and innovation.
- Risk is quantifiable; uncertainty is unquantifiable and unpredictable.
- Market research can allow businesses to understand the customers to whom they plan to sell, enabling better marketing decisions to be made.
- Market research can gather fresh information (primary) or be based on information already gathered (secondary).
- Market research can be carried out on a large enough scale to give statistically reliable results

- (quantitative) or can be small scale, in-depth and designed to give insights (qualitative).
- Market research methods can undermine the reliability of research results if sample sizes are small or samples are poorly selected.
- ICT can help gather and analyse market research data.
- Market research can help to segment markets.
- Market mapping helps to make decisions over where to try to position a product in the market.
- Successful market mapping requires good decisions on what to plot on the map's axes and where to place existing products.
- Having some kind of competitive advantage is crucial for the success of any product.
- Competitive advantage can come from lowest costs or product differentiation.
- Differentiation may be tangible or perceived.
- Differentiation helps to lessen the effects of competitors' actions, allows firms greater price flexibility and helps to add value to products and services.

3 The market

Demand

Demand is such a fundamental concept in business that understanding the factors that affect demand is critical to running a successful business. The main factors affecting demand are listed below.

> **Demand** is the term used to describe the level of interest customers have in a product.

Price

REVISED

Higher prices lead to lower **effective demand**, since fewer customers can afford to pay. Price also affects consumers' decisions on relative value of the product compared to alternatives – higher prices make alternatives seem better value. On the other hand, prices give off a signal about the product being sold – so lower prices may damage consumer perceptions of quality.

> **Effective demand** is interest backed by the ability to pay.

Changes in prices of substitutes and complements

REVISED

A clear relationship exists between demand for a product and the price of its **substitutes**. If the price of a tin of *Roses* falls, demand for *Quality Street* will fall as consumers switch to buying the cheaper substitute. The same relationship holds if the price of the substitute rises; demand for *Quality Street* will increase as consumers switch away from *Roses*, the more expensive substitute.

The relationship between demand for a product and the price of its **complements** works in the other direction. Should the price of a complementary product rise, demand for the original product is likely to fall. Often complementary products can represent the 'running costs' of another product, such as petrol for cars, or coffee capsules for coffee machines. If the price of the complementary product rises, demand for the original will fall, and vice versa.

> A **substitute** is a similar, rival product that consumers may choose instead.
>
> A **complement** is a product whose use accompanies another, so petrol is a complementary product to cars.

> **Typical mistake**
>
> Too many candidates under pressure confuse the terms 'complement' and 'substitute' – pause before choosing the appropriate term.

Changes in consumer incomes

REVISED

As income levels rise, demand for most products (normal goods) rises in line, as consumers have more income to spend. For luxury goods such as Porsche cars, demand will rise even faster than incomes. Of course, incomes do not always rise. As economies go through recession, incomes will fall, and for normal and luxury goods, demand falls as consumers try to save money. However, some products, known as inferior goods, see demand rise when incomes fall, as happened to Poundland in the recession-affected years 2008–13. Inferior goods, as their name suggests, tend to be cheaper alternatives to normal goods, which consumers can switch to in order to save money when their income is falling. As incomes rise again, consumers will switch back to normal and luxury goods, leading to a fall in demand for inferior goods.

Fashions, tastes and preferences

Subject to change over time, factors such as attitudes to diet (for example, no sugar or low fat) change unpredictably but can have a major impact upon demand for products, either positive or negative.

Advertising and branding

Successful advertising can lead to major short-term increases in demand. Consistent advertising linked to other marketing activity may help to build a brand, protecting it from direct competition and making sales volumes relatively stable.

Demographics

Changes in the make-up of populations, which form the basis of any market's demand, can affect demand for individual products. Major demographic trends in the UK in recent years have seen a growing population of over-60s, a rising birth rate and increased numbers of European migrants. All these groups provide opportunities for increased demand for carefully targeted products.

External shocks

Natural disasters, changes in the law, unexpected traffic problems or a major customer not renewing a contract are all examples of events that can have a hugely damaging impact on demand for small or large businesses. The major problem with many external shocks is their unpredictability. They are outside the business's control.

Seasonality

Seasonal factors affect demand for many products, whether they are related to the weather and nature's seasons or due to special events during the course of a year, such as Christmas.

Now test yourself

1 List seven factors that could affect demand for a product.
2 If the price of petrol falls, what is likely to happen to demand for cars?
3 If the price of Adidas trainers increases, what is likely to happen to demand for Nike trainers?
4 Give two examples of external shocks that could damage demand for a local independent coffee shop.

Answers on p. 121

Supply

Along with demand, the amount that businesses are willing and able to supply will have a major impact on the price of all products. The general rule governing the amount firms are willing to supply is that the more profit they can make by supplying a product, the more they are willing to supply. This is because firms making choices over how to use the resources they have available are assumed to put those resources to whatever use will maximise profit for them.

Changes in costs of production

REVISED

If the cost of making a product changes, the amount that a business is willing to supply will adjust accordingly:
● If production costs rise, the amount supplied will fall.
● If production costs fall, the amount supplied will rise.

This is because as costs rise and fall, the amount of profit the firm can make changes. Firms will always supply more if they can make more profit and less if profits are lower.

The most common cause of changed production costs is changes in the costs of the resources used to make a product, including materials and labour.

Introduction of new technology

REVISED

New technology used in production, such as industrial robots, tends to reduce the costs of production:
● The introduction of new technology should lead to an increase in supply.

Not only are firms willing to supply more with lower production costs offering higher profits, but also new production technology may increase capacity, meaning that there is more output available.

Indirect taxes

REVISED

Indirect taxes act just like another component of the cost of producing a product or service. Therefore:
● An increase in indirect tax rates will increase cost and therefore reduce supply.
● A decrease in indirect tax rates will cut total costs and therefore increase supply.

> **Indirect taxes** are taxes that the government imposes on goods and services, for example VAT.

Government subsidies

REVISED

These are the opposite of taxes. When the government wants to encourage the supply of a product such as wind-powered energy, it may offer subsidies to businesses. This cuts the cost of production faced by the business, meaning that subsidies will increase supply.

External shocks

REVISED

Unexpected events such as economic crises, poor harvests or natural disasters can reduce the total quantity of an item available. This would lead to an increase in the price of the item, meaning that production costs rise and firms reduce the amount they are willing to supply.

Now test yourself

TESTED

5 Explain the relationship between costs of production and supply.
6 How might the invention of a new, more efficient production robot affect the supply of cars?
7 Give an example of an external shock that may reduce the supply of wheat.
8 Explain two reasons why governments might offer subsidies to firms supplying wind turbines.
9 What would be the effect of a reduction in the rate of VAT on supply?

Answers on pp. 121–2

Markets and equilibrium

The interaction of supply and demand

REVISED

In **commodity markets**, price is determined simply by the interaction of supply and demand. Simply stated:

● If demand is higher than supply, the price of the product will rise, until demand falls back to the level of supply.
● If supply is higher than demand, price will fall, stimulating more demand to ensure that all that is supplied is sold.

What is happening is that price adjusts until demand and supply are in **equilibrium**. This is the natural state for all markets in which price is determined simply by demand and supply.

Commodity markets are markets for undifferentiated products, generally raw materials such as gold, crude oil or rice.

Equilibrium describes a situation in a market where supply and demand are balanced, making the price stable.

Supply and demand diagrams

REVISED

Drawing a demand curve simply involves plotting a series of points showing how much of a product would be demanded at a range of different price levels. In a similar way, a supply curve can be plotted, showing how much of a product businesses are willing to supply at a range of price levels.

Table 3.1 shows the demand and supply of sacks of coffee beans at a range of prices.

Table 3.1 Demand and supply of sacks of coffee beans

Price ($ per sack)	Demand (million sacks)	Supply (million sacks)
210	175	125
230	165	140
250	155	155
270	145	170
290	135	185

This information can be used to plot both a demand curve and a supply curve on a diagram that will show the market for coffee beans (Figure 3.1).

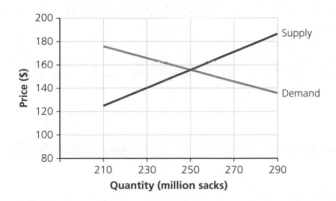

Figure 3.1 Equilibrium in the market for coffee beans

As Figure 3.1 clearly shows, the current equilibrium price is at $250 per sack, i.e. the place at which the level of demand and supply are the same.

If there is a significant change in the factors that determine the demand or supply of coffee, the lines will change. Possible reasons for these changes are examined on pages 17–19. These will cause leftward or rightward shifts in the demand and supply curves. They will need to be redrawn and are likely to generate a new equilibrium price. Table 3.2 summarises the effect on price of shifts in the curves.

Table 3.2 Effect on price of shifts in the demand/supply curves

If this changes	Price will move
Demand curve moves to the right (rises)	up
Demand curve moves to the left (falls)	down
Supply curve moves to the left (falls)	up
Supply curve moves to the right (rises)	down

Now test yourself

TESTED

10 What name is given to products that cannot be differentiated?
11 Why does a demand curve slope downwards from left to right?
12 Why does a supply curve slope upwards from left to right?
13 What name is given to the point at which demand and supply curves cross?
14 State two factors that may cause a demand curve to shift.
15 State two factors that may cause a supply curve to shift.

Answers on p. 122

Price elasticity of demand

Price elasticity of demand measures the responsiveness of demand for a product to a change in its price.

Calculation

REVISED

Price elasticity of demand can be calculated by measuring the percentage change in demand that follows a change in price:

$$\text{Price elasticity of demand} = \frac{\% \text{ change in demand}}{\% \text{ change in price}}$$

Interpreting price elasticity

REVISED

Once elasticity has been calculated, the result can be interpreted, as shown in Table 3.3.

Table 3.3 Differences between price elasticity and inelasticity

If price elasticity is between 0 and −1	If price elasticity is a negative number greater than 1
Product is price inelastic	Product is price elastic
Changes in price have proportionately smaller effect on demand/sales	Changes in price have a proportionately larger effect on sales/demand

Price elasticity and revenue

REVISED

Depending on a product's price elasticity it is possible to make definitive statements about the effect of price changes on its revenue (Table 3.4).

Table 3.4 Price elasticity and revenue

If the product is:	Change in price:	Effect on revenue:	Explanation:
Price elastic	Increasing price	Fall in revenue	Because a small increase in price leads to a large fall in demand
Price elastic	Decreasing price	Increases revenue	Because a small cut in price leads to a large increase in demand
Price inelastic	Increasing price	Increases revenue	Because an increase in price leads to a small fall in demand
Price inelastic	Decreasing price	Fall in revenue	Because a price cut will only cause a small increase in demand

This predictability gives the opportunity to generate clear advice to offer in answer to questions asking for recommendations about a product's selling price.

Factors influencing price elasticity

REVISED

The major factors affecting price elasticity all boil down to whether the product seems different to its rivals. They are:
- degree of product differentiation
- availability of direct substitutes
- branding and brand loyalty.

Ultimately the issue is whether customers go into a shop seeking out *Marmite* or *Heinz Ketchup*, or whether they'll scan the shelves making price comparisons to decide what to buy. If price is a central factor in the decision, price elasticity will be high ('elastic'). If it's got to be *Nike*, price elasticity will be low ('inelastic').

Significance of price elasticity

REVISED

Price elasticity is a useful concept for managers for two major reasons:
- Price elasticity can help in forecasting sales, by considering the likely impact of planned future price changes.
- Knowledge of price elasticity can help to decide on the best pricing strategy for increasing revenue, as shown in Table 3.4 above.

However, it is important to consider that price elasticity values tend to change over time since in a competitive market many firms' actions will affect the extent to which one product stands out from its rivals (just think how many chocolate bars there are). This unpredictability can undermine the usefulness of price elasticity by making it hard to really know the current price elasticity until after price has been changed and the effect on demand measured.

> **Exam tip**
>
> Most businesses prefer to have price inelastic products because they are able to increase their price if necessary as a result of perhaps an increase in costs. This helps to explain why so much marketing activity can be traced back to attempts to make the product stand out from its rivals, reducing price elasticity.

Now test yourself

TESTED

16 Would a well-known popular branded product be likely to be price elastic or inelastic?
17 To increase revenue on a price elastic product, should price be increased or decreased?
18 What three factors determine price elasticity?
19 What are the two major uses of price elasticity for marketing managers?
20 What is the major limitation to the use of price elasticity?

Answers on p. 122

Income elasticity of demand

Income elasticity of demand measures the responsiveness of demand for a product to a change in **real incomes**.

> **Real income** is the amount by which average incomes have adjusted for inflation – the amount by which prices have risen. For example: average household incomes up 3% in the past year; inflation at 1.2% – so real incomes are up by 3% – 1.2% = 1.8%.

Calculating income elasticity

REVISED

Income elasticity of demand can be calculated by measuring the percentage change in demand that follows a change in real incomes:

$$\text{Income elasticity of demand} = \frac{\%\text{ change in demand}}{\%\text{ change in real incomes}}$$

Typical mistake

Unlike calculations of price elasticity, the result of an income elasticity calculation can be either positive or negative. It is important to make sure you pay attention to whether the changes in demand and income are positive or negative and carefully note the sign of your answer. This will determine how the product is categorised.

Typical mistake

Always use percentage change figures. Do not simply use the absolute changes in income (£s) or demand (units sold).

Interpreting income elasticity

REVISED

When categorising products and services according to their income elasticity there are three possible types:
- Inferior goods: These will have a negative income elasticity.
- Normal goods: These are products with a positive income elasticity between 0 and 1.
- Luxury goods: These goods and services have a positive income elasticity that is greater than 1.

Table 3.5 Effect of changes in income on different types of product

Type of product	Change in real incomes	Change in demand	Explanation
Inferior good	Increase	Decrease	Consumers stop buying cheaper substitutes and trade up now they have more money
	Decrease	Increase	Consumers switch to these products to save money as their incomes fall
Normal good	Increase	Increase at the same rate as real income or a little slower	Increasingly affluent consumers are now able to buy a little more of this type of product
	Decrease	Decrease at the same rate as real income or a little slower	As consumers tighten their belts, they will cut back a little on these products
Luxury good	Increase	Increase at a faster rate than real incomes	As consumers' incomes rise, these luxuries are the ones that most of their extra income will be spent on
	Decrease	Decrease at a faster rate than real incomes	These will be the first products to disappear from consumers' shopping baskets when they feel the need to tighten their belts

Factors affecting income elasticity

REVISED

Necessity or indulgence?

The indulgences – those things we can easily live without, but love to treat ourselves to when we can afford to – will be those that are most sensitive to changes in income. Necessities are those more basic items that we would always expect to buy, even when times are tight, therefore they are not as sensitive to changes in real incomes. Although we may try to cut back on the amount of pasta we buy when times are tight, we will continue to buy it.

Exam practice answers and quick quizzes at **www.hoddereducation.co.uk/myrevisionnotes**

Who buys the product?

The super-rich will still be able to afford to buy luxuries even during a recession, so demand for Bugatti cars may well be unaffected, whereas demand for Porsche sports cars may fall as those who are 'merely rich' need to cut back on some of their luxuries.

Significance of income elasticity

Sales forecasting

Knowledge of the likely reaction of a product to a change in real incomes allows a business to forecast sales *if* it has reliable economic forecasts available. Of course, the reliability of economic forecasts is not always strong.

> **Typical mistake**
>
> Income elasticities change over time. As a result, a company can never be 100% confident that what happened to sales last time real incomes changed will be repeated. Add to this the fact that most economic forecasts tend to be a little inaccurate (at best) and writing about using elasticity to forecast sales should be accompanied by words such as 'may' or 'could' instead of 'will'.

Financial planning

If income elasticity gives sales forecasts, then this information can be factored into budgets and financial plans. If a recession is forecast, a firm producing luxuries can plan ways to reduce costs in advance of a probable sharp fall in sales.

Product portfolio management

Having a product portfolio consisting entirely of luxuries *or* inferior goods increases the danger of changes in real income having a critical impact on sales. Firms intending to spread their risk will look to ensure that their product portfolios contain products with a range of income elasticities. Though this may sound easy, it can be hard for a business selling a luxury good to prevent damage to its image if it releases an inferior version.

> **Now test yourself**
>
> TESTED
>
> 21 If average earnings rise by 4% and prices rise by 2.5%, what is the change in real income?
>
> 22 If a 3% fall in real income leads to a 6% rise in demand for potatoes, what is their income elasticity?
>
> 23 What are the two main factors affecting the income elasticity of a product?
>
> 24 State two reasons why sales forecasts based on income elasticity may prove inaccurate.
>
> 25 What name is given to a product with a negative income elasticity?
>
> 26 Will the demand for a product go up or down if:
>   (a) The price of a substitute rises
>   (b) The price of a substitute falls
>   (c) The price of a complementary good rises
>   (d) The price of a complementary good falls?
>
> Answers on p. 122

Exam practice

The UK market for milk

Demand and supply of milk in the UK at different price levels

Price (pence per litre)	Demand (billion litres)	Supply (billion litres)
42	15.0	14.0
43	14.8	14.3
44	14.6	14.6
45	14.4	14.9
46	14.2	15.2

The estimated income elasticity of milk in the UK is +0.1.

Questions

1 On one diagram, draw a demand and supply curve for milk in the UK using the data in the table above. (4)
2 Using the data in the table for demand at a price of 44p per litre and 45p per litre, calculate the price elasticity of demand for milk. (3)
3 Calculate the impact on demand for milk in the UK if incomes fell by 5% in a year, if price was 42p per litre. (3)
4 Explain two possible factors affecting supply of milk in the UK. (10)

Answers and quick quiz 3 online

ONLINE

Summary

- In addition to price there are seven other major factors that could affect demand for a product. They are:
  - changes in the prices of substitutes and complementary goods
  - changes in consumer incomes
  - fashions, tastes and preferences
  - advertising and branding
  - demographics
  - external shocks
  - seasonality.
- Decisions on how much to supply are governed by how much profit a business can make.
- Changes that would increase the amount of profit a firm can make lead to an increased willingness to supply and vice versa.
- The major factors affecting supply in most markets are: changes in the costs of production, introduction of new technology, indirect taxes, government subsidies, external shocks.
- In markets with undifferentiated products, price is determined by the interaction of demand and supply.
- A demand curve shows the amount of the product that would be demanded at a range of price levels.
- A supply curve shows the amount of a product that firms would be willing to supply at different price levels.

- The point where the two curves cross is the equilibrium position, i.e. the point at which the price will be stable in the short term.
- Demand and supply curves shift due to a range of different causes.
- Shifts in demand or supply cause changes in the equilibrium price in a market.
- Price elasticity measures the responsiveness of demand to a change in price.
- All price elasticities are negative values.
- Price inelastic products have an elasticity between 0 and −1.
- Price elastic products are those with a price elasticity greater than −1.
- Price elasticity depends on the extent to which a product stands out from its rivals.
- Increasing the price of a price inelastic product will lead to an increase in revenue.
- Income elasticity of demand

  $$= \frac{\% \text{ change in demand}}{\% \text{ change in real incomes}}$$

- According to their income elasticity, products are classified as luxury goods, normal goods or inferior goods.
- Income elasticity depends on whether the product is an indulgence or a necessity and on who buys the product.
- Income elasticity information can be used to forecast sales, aid financial planning and design a balanced product portfolio.

4 Marketing mix and strategy

The marketing mix is the collective term for the four major marketing decisions that a firm faces when trying to build a coherent plan, or strategy, for how its product will be marketed. Each of the Ps (product, place, promotion and price) should work in harmony to generate a coherent, credible image for the product

Product and service design

Design is everywhere – any product that has been made has been designed, including products that are used to make other products. Services are also designed, perhaps in a less obvious way and using slightly different principles from, say, designing a sports car. The process by which services are purchased also has to be planned and therefore designed – perhaps designing an easy-to-use, attractive-looking app for ordering that pizza. So the principles of the design mix still apply.

The design mix
REVISED

Design is a compromise. Product and service designers must consider each of the points of the triangle in Figure 4.1.

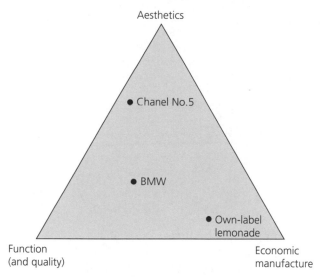

Figure 4.1 The design mix

- *Aesthetics* is the word used to describe the look, taste, texture or feel of an item.
- *Function* relates to whether the item actually does what it is expected to do and the extent to which it surpasses expectations of quality of performance.
- *Economic manufacture* considers the ease and economy with which the item can actually be made on the scale required.

However, for many firms, one aspect will take priority over the other two, so own-label drinks manufacturers will be far more concerned about designing a product that can be manufactured very cheaply than quality or aesthetics. However, not all businesses will head for the edges. As can be seen, BMW tries to strike a fine balance between all three aspects of the mix.

Benefits of good design

REVISED

- Can add value
- Can provide a point of differentiation
- Can reduce manufacturing costs, boosting profit margins
- Improves brand image
- May boost brand loyalty

Changes in the design mix to reflect social trends

REVISED

Environmental concerns

As acceptance of the need to be aware of the environmental impact of business activity grows, product design has increasingly focused on three key environmental concerns:
- **Sustainability**: This is the need to ensure that materials and components used are sustainably sourced.
- Design for waste minimisation or reuse: This describes a growing awareness of the need to design products from the outset with the end of their lives in mind. Designers are trying to ensure that the parts of a product that cannot be reused and must be thrown away are reduced to as close to zero as possible.
- Recycling: Even those parts of products that cannot be reused may be able to be recycled for another use. Wherever possible many designers are now looking to ensure recyclability of products and components.

> **Sustainability** means making something using materials that will still be available in the future, perhaps because you plant one tree for every one you cut down.

Ethical sourcing

Media coverage over recent years has begun to examine the sources of components and finished goods used by businesses. Reports of child labour being used to make clothing, or unethical fishing methods used to catch tuna, have encouraged designers to ensure that the components or ingredients used in their products come from ethical sources.

Now test yourself

TESTED

1 What are the three points of the design mix?
2 What type of business may be most concerned with economy of manufacture?
3 State three possible benefits to a business of great design.
4 List three environmental concerns increasingly considered in product design.
5 How can design help to ensure ethical sourcing?

Answers on p. 122

Branding and promotion

Both branding and **promotion** are methods of communicating, explicitly or implicitly, information about a product or service to consumers.

> **Promotion** describes methods used by the business to communicate information and persuade consumers to purchase a product.

Types of promotion

These are best categorised into two groups: those that are aimed at boosting sales in the long term and those that are simply expected to generate a short-term effect.

Long-term methods

- Persuasive advertising
- **Public relations**

Short-term methods

- Buy one get one free (BOGOF)
- Seasonal price-cutting promotions

> **Public relations** describes attempts by a business to create publicity that is reported as news, such as staging a glitzy launch party for a new product.

> **Exam tip**
>
> Think carefully when answering a question about an appropriate form of promotion. Ask yourself about the goals of the business: a short-term boost in sales? Or are they willing to invest in long-term sales growth?

Types of branding

Individual brand

These are single product **brands**, such as *Marmite* or *Penguin* (biscuits). The firm that manufactures these brands may make little or no attempt to push their company name, focusing instead on the single brand to provide focus. Which company makes *Penguins*? And which makes *Marmite*?

> A **brand** is a recognisable name or logo that helps to differentiate a product or business.

Brand family

This is a brand name that is used across a range of related products, with Cadbury being a prime example. The benefit of this is the ability to use the umbrella brand name to encourage sales of each product within the family through association with others. A strong brand family also makes it much easier to get retail distribution when launching new products.

Corporate brand

Using the company name as a brand, in the way that Nestlé does, can convince consumers that all products across the entire range share similar benefits (or drawbacks!). Even for Nestlé, though, there may be individual products that seem stronger without the corporate brand logo, such as Nespresso (a Nestlé innovation that keeps quiet about the brand connection).

Ways to build a brand

- Advertising: This works best as a way of reinforcing the messages the company wants to send about its brand.
- **Unique selling point (USP)**: This may well provide the key stimulus that launches a brand, and although the unique feature may be copied in time, the brand may already be well established before this happens.
- Sponsorship: This is a way of brand building by association. Sponsoring an event, a sports team or even a TV programme can help to create

> A **unique selling point (USP)** is a particular feature of a product or service that no rival provides.

attachments in consumers' minds that build the brand's personality: for example, Red Bull sponsoring extreme sports.

● Digital media: From using social media to build relationships with customers to using Google Adwords to pop up every time a particular search is carried out, digital media offer a range of methods to help build a brand, some of which have not even been developed yet.

Changes in branding and promotion to reflect social trends

REVISED

Viral marketing

Traditionally, businesses loved creating 'word of mouth' promotion, where happy customers recommended a business to their friends and family – the good reputation of the business was spread like a virus. In a digital world, word of mouth became supercharged, with social media offering a faster and wider way to spread good (and bad) recommendations about a product.

Social media

Social media, just like traditional media (TV, newspapers), are seen by many businesses as another place where they can display their promotional messages, through an Instagram or Snapchat account, on a Facebook page or a Twitter feed.

Emotional branding

In some ways all branding is attempting to create some kind of emotional response from consumers to the brand. However, some branding is more overtly emotional than others; think about the sense of fun created by Ben and Jerry's. With the advent of digital media, especially social media, the relationship between a brand and a consumer can reach new emotional levels, with consumers following certain brands for daily updates from their brand of choice.

Now test yourself

TESTED

6 State two forms of promotion that may provide a short-term boost in sales but undermine a firm's brand image.
7 Give one disadvantage that can arise from creating a corporate brand.
8 List three methods that can be used effectively to build a brand.
9 Explain why viral marketing has become more significant in recent years.

Answers on p. 122

Pricing strategies

When making decisions on how to decide price for a product, a business is likely to devise a general approach to pricing, such as Apple pricing high to 'confirm' the brand's superiority and to complement other aspects of the marketing mix. Short-term changes in price may occasionally be prompted by external events, but in the medium to long term a company's pricing strategy shapes decisions on the actual price to charge.

Types of pricing strategy

For NEW products

Price skimming

This involves launching a brand new product at a high price while the product is unique.

Penetration

This involves launching a new product at a very low price to entice customers to try it.

> **Exam tip**
>
> The decision over pricing strategy for new products must be determined by the level of competition. A new product that has no clear rivals is likely to use skimming, but a product with many close competitors cannot use skimming as nobody would be likely to buy. Before deciding on a sensible pricing strategy, ask how unique the product is.

Table 4.1 Advantages and disadvantages of price skimming and price penetration

	Price skimming	**Price penetration**
Advantages	● High prices help to create a desirable image for the product ● Early adopters will pay the high price in return for exclusivity ● High prices generate rapid profits – helping to recover the costs of innovation quickly	● Low prices encourage lower-risk product sampling ● Low prices boost sale volumes – cutting production costs ● High volumes may persuade retailers to buy the product – boosting distribution ● Encourages customers to develop the habit of buying the product
Disadvantages	● Will deter some customers with price seen as a 'rip-off' ● Early buyers may be frustrated once price starts to fall ● Image may suffer when prices begin to fall	● Product's image may be immediately cast as 'cheap' ● Upmarket retailers may be unwilling to stock the product ● Likely to create price sensitivity among customers – a higher price elasticity

For EXISTING products

Cost-plus

This involves deciding price by adding a desired percentage onto total costs per unit:

Price charged = unit cost + (% mark-up)
- Benefit: This should guarantee a profit is made on each unit sold.
- Drawback: Ignoring the market may mean an unrealistic price is generated.
- Appropriate: When the firm is a market leader with little need to worry about competition.

Predatory

A strategy that sets price low enough to force a competitor out of business – often only on a local basis where competitors are smaller, local firms.
- Benefit: Once a rival has been forced to close, prices can be pushed up higher, increasing margins.
- Drawback: If it can be proven to be specifically designed only to drive rivals out of business, predatory pricing is illegal.
- Appropriate: When a firm is clearly more financially powerful than smaller rivals.

Competitive

A competitive pricing strategy means charging a price at the market average or at a discount to the average price in the market.
- Benefit: This should ensure that price will not put customers off buying the product.
- Drawback: Firms that use a competitive pricing strategy have little control over the price they charge and thus the revenue they generate.
- Appropriate: When a company is trying to take on more powerful rivals.

Psychological

Less of a strategy and more of a tactic used to make fine-tuned decisions on the price to charge, prices are set just below major psychological levels, such as £9.99 instead of £10, or £9,995 instead of £10,000.
- Advantage: This can help nudge customers into making a purchase by helping them to believe they are not quite spending £10 or £10,000.
- Drawback: It may have little effect on many planned purchases and may in fact mildly annoy consumers.
- Appropriate: When selling impulse purchases or 'little treats'.

Factors that determine the most appropriate pricing strategy

REVISED

- Level of product differentiation: Highly differentiated products will have more control over pricing, potentially allowing them to use cost-plus pricing.
- Price elasticity of demand: Inelastic demand means that firms can adjust prices however they wish without seeing major impacts on demand, whereas a producer of a price elastic product will always face pressure to reduce prices in order to boost demand and may be unable even to contemplate an increase in price. This pushes them into a competitive pricing strategy.
- Level of competition: The higher the level of competition, the less scope a firm has for moving away from a purely competitive strategy.
- Strength of brand: Strong brands differentiate products, reducing their price elasticity. This all adds up to the ability to take control over their own pricing, probably allowing a cost-plus approach.
- Stage in the product life cycle: During the introduction phase there's a key decision to make – penetration or skimming; pricing will often change, perhaps being pushed up as the product moves through growth and into maturity.
- Costs and the need to make a profit: As price has a direct impact on revenue, a business has to consider its costs when deciding price. Pricing below unit costs will lead to loss-making, which is

unsustainable in the long term. However, a balance must be struck between pushing price above costs to maximise profit and ensuring that the price is relatively competitive.

Changes in pricing to reflect social trends

- Online sales: pricing online may be more sensitive than on the high street because online consumers find it easier to compare prices than those trudging around different stores. Pricing levels may be lower as running an online business generates lower fixed costs than 'bricks and mortar' stores that have rents to cover in prime locations.
- Price comparison sites appear to encourage firms to price competitively so their products and services show up as best value on these sites. In fact, though, many of these sites are simply sales outlets for producers; consumers should beware of assuming they are being told about the best deals available.

Now test yourself

TESTED

10 Why would a firm launching a copycat product into a competitive market be wrong to choose price skimming as a pricing strategy?
11 Why might a luxury brand avoid penetration pricing for new products?
12 To calculate price using cost-plus pricing, a percentage mark-up is added on to what?
13 What level of market share are firms using competitive pricing likely to have?
14 Why does the absence of a strong brand name on a product suggest competitive pricing is a sensible choice?
15 A bakery makes 600 hot cross buns for Easter Saturday. Each bun has 4p of ingredients, 3p of labour and will go into a 1p bag. The energy cost for the 600 buns is £24 and the mark-up is 200% on unit cost. Using cost-plus pricing, what is the selling price per bun?

Answers on p. 122

Distribution

Place, or distribution, is a vital part of the marketing mix, because if consumers cannot get access to the product, they will not be able to buy it.

Typical mistake

Too many answers show naivety in implying that any manufacturing business can get their product into any retailer. Especially for small businesses, securing distribution for their product can be one of their biggest challenges. In the UK a huge proportion of grocery items are sold through four supermarket chains. *If* a manufacturer can convince one of the big four to sell its product, that may be the key to success. However, with limited space available on supermarket shelves, the level of competition for that space is huge.

The route a product takes from producer to consumer is called the **distribution channel**.

Intermediaries are businesses between the producer and the consumer in a distribution channel, such as retailers.

Distribution channels

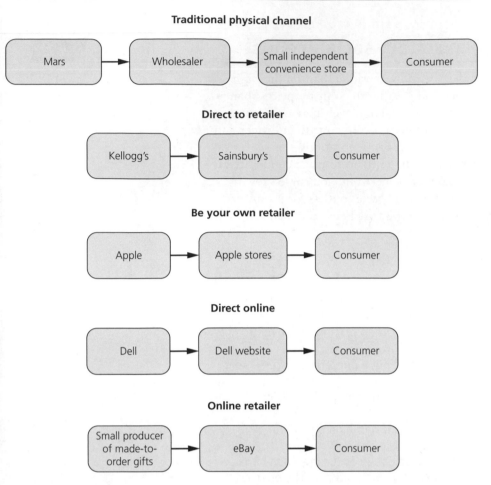

Traditional physical channel

Mars → Wholesaler → Small independent convenience store → Consumer

Direct to retailer

Kellogg's → Sainsbury's → Consumer

Be your own retailer

Apple → Apple stores → Consumer

Direct online

Dell → Dell website → Consumer

Online retailer

Small producer of made-to-order gifts → eBay → Consumer

Figure 4.2 Examples of distribution channels

Traditional physical channel

Many producers sell their products to wholesalers who act as suppliers to smaller retailers. This channel pushes selling prices up as wholesalers and retailers will both add their own markup. However, this channel helps smaller firms to achieve a wide distribution across many outlets.

Direct to retailer

Larger producers can ignore wholesalers and sell their products in bulk to major retail chains, saving on the wholesalers' markup but exposing them to tough negotiations with retail chains on price and credit terms.

Be your own retailer

Producers that want to exert complete control over how their products are sold can set up their own retail outlets. Apple stores are designed to showcase Apple products in the best possible environment to show their strengths, but this of course means Apple incurs significant costs running these stores.

Direct online

Producers can set up their own websites – often at significant cost – to allow consumers to buy products directly from them. This means the producer keeps the full price paid but it excludes the possibility of selling to consumers who are uncomfortable buying online.

Online retail

For smaller producers unable to afford the expense of building slick e-commerce platforms, existing sites, most notably eBay, offer the chance to sell online to a wide audience without the same investment, but with the disadvantage of eBay's fee.

Changes in distribution to reflect social trends

REVISED

Online

Direct channels of distribution are not new. Mail order and catalogues have been around for over 50 years. The difference that direct online distribution makes is in the power of websites to offer a wide and varied range of products, with the scope to update the product on a daily basis. In addition, online distribution offers small firms the chance to reach a global audience in a way that other channels simply could not offer.

From product to service

Some services will never be distributed online, or in any other way than the provider and the customer meeting face to face. Haircuts, clubbing or staying in a hotel will always involve personal interaction, even if the way you book changes over time. From booking face to face at a travel agent, to booking a holiday by phone, time moves on and now online holiday booking sites dominate the industry.

Now test yourself

TESTED

16 Briefly explain why getting the 'place' element of the marketing mix wrong can destroy a product's chances of success.
17 Explain the role of wholesalers in a traditional channel of distribution.
18 Identify one benefit and one drawback to a producer of opening its own retail outlets.
19 How has the growth of e-commerce helped small producers?

Answers on pp. 122–3

Product life cycle and portfolio

The product life cycle

REVISED

The product life cycle is a pattern of sales over time that most products tend to follow. The life cycle model has four phases following the launch of a product:

● Introduction
● Growth
● Maturity
● Decline

Sometimes an additional phase – development – is identified as happening before the product is launched.

Each phase is characterised by what is happening to sales of the product (Table 4.2).

Table 4.2 Phases of the product life cycle

Introduction	Sales are low and rise only slowly
Growth	Sales begin to rise much more quickly
Maturity	Growth in sales now slows and sales stabilise at their highest level
Decline	During this phase sales of the product begin to fall, until the product is phased out or an extension strategy is launched

The key decision-making benefit of the product life cycle model is to help make effective marketing decisions. Examples include pricing decisions and advertising spending.

Issues with the product life cycle

Decision-makers using the product life cycle model to help them select appropriate marketing activities have a problem. Though the model seems to predict the future, sometimes the decisions made by the marketing bosses can actually move a product from one phase of the life cycle to the next.

For example:
- The manager of an existing brand in maturity expects the product to go into decline.
- If the latest sales figures show a dip in sales, the manager may decide this shows the decline phase has begun.
- They may therefore slash the amount spent on promoting the product, as the model suggests is appropriate for products in decline.
- This itself may lead to a sustained reduction in sales and may have actually hastened the decline of the product.

This chain of events shows how the life cycle model itself may encourage managers to make decisions that speed a product through the life cycle faster than might naturally occur otherwise.

Extension strategies

REVISED

Of course, many businesses faced with a product nearing the end of its maturity stage or even entering the decline stage may be keen to squeeze more life out of their product. Changes can be made to the product's marketing mix that provide not just a quick burst of sales but a medium- to long-term effect of sales – preventing decline or even boosting sales.

The two major adjustments that can lead to successful **extension strategies** are shown in Table 4.3.

> An **extension strategy** is a medium- to long-term plan for extending the life cycle of a product.

Table 4.3 Changes that can lead to successful extension strategies

Changes to the product	• Adding extra functions or features • Changing ingredients/materials • Launching slightly different variants on the product – shapes/sizes, etc.
Changes to promotion (not simply a new advertising campaign)	• Targeting a different market segment • Finding new uses for the product • Increasing use of the product among existing customers

Exam tip

An extension strategy is an attempt to solve a business problem. As with all problem-solving, the best solutions will always address the specific causes of the problem. Recognising whether this is happening in a case study offers excellent scope for evaluation.

New product development

Developing new products is the key to long-term success for most businesses. Unfortunately, the process is both expensive and time-consuming. In addition, it is fraught with possibilities of failure. The processes involved in developing a new product or service may include:

- Research and development
- Market research
- Product design
- Product engineering
- Packaging design
- Advertising
- Pricing
- Branding

A general rule of thumb suggests that only one in five new products actually becomes commercially successful.

The major issues that are likely to determine the success of a new product are:

- Understanding the needs and wants of the market
- The creativity with which solutions to problems can be found
- Finding and committing the resources (money and people) needed for the new product development to succeed

The product portfolio

Large businesses normally sell a range (or portfolio) of different products. A company such as Unilever sells a wide range of products including:

- Comfort
- Domestos
- Dove
- Hellman's
- Flora
- Knorr
- Lynx
- Magnum
- Sure
- Persil
- Brut
- Cif
- Cornetto
- I can't believe it's not butter

With such a wide range of different brands and products to manage, it is important that Unilever marketing managers continually develop new products and kill off those products whose sales are falling – and consequently draining resources that could be better used on other products within their portfolio. In order to manage their portfolio of brands successfully, marketing managers will analyse their product portfolio regularly, often using a tool called the Boston Matrix.

The Boston Matrix

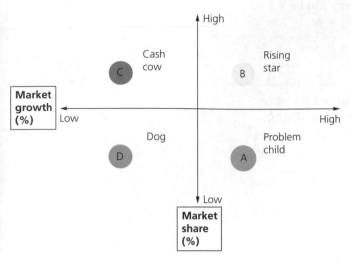

Figure 4.3 The Boston Matrix

The matrix assesses each product within a firm's product portfolio. The two key variables considered are market share and growth of the market in which the product is being sold. Once these two figures have been discovered, each product in the portfolio can be plotted on the axes shown in Figure 4.3.

Each quadrant of the diagram above is labelled with a memorable tag:
● Problem child
● Rising star
● Cash cow
● Dog

Typical characteristics of each type of product are shown in Table 4.4.

Table 4.4 Typical characteristics of the Boston Matrix categories

Problem child	These products may be successful in the future but currently have low market share. Their potential, however, is based on the fact that they are being sold in rapidly growing markets offering the chance of rapid sales growth if supported by the right marketing.
Rising star	These are products in exciting and rapidly growing markets that currently hold a high share and are the future money-makers for the firm. Although these products will need a lot of money spent on them at the moment – fighting off all the competitors attracted to these high growth markets – if high share can be maintained, future profitability is likely.
Cash cows	These are products in stable markets that hold a high share, and can therefore generate relatively high sales with relatively low marketing expenditure. As a result they are likely to generate significant profits that the business can use to help further develop other products within its portfolio.
Dogs	These products have a low share of a low growth market and are thus generally unattractive members of the portfolio. They are the most likely candidates to be killed off.

Now test yourself

TESTED ☐

20 List the four stages of the product life cycle.
21 What is the stage of the life cycle sometimes called before a product is launched?
22 What are the three main influences on the success of the new product development process?
23 What four labels are given to the four quarters of the Boston Matrix?

Answers on p. 123

Marketing strategy

Successful **marketing strategy** is likely to be characterised in three ways:

- Strategy is about the future: Success in most markets relies on predicting the future market conditions and ensuring that the plan devised for marketing the business's products suits the market conditions that will develop during the life of the strategy.
- Strategy must be achievable: Not only must a strategy use only the resources the firm can call upon to deliver its marketing plans, but also the plans themselves must address the real conditions operating within the market, for example operating within an economic downturn.
- Strategy is company specific: There is usually only space in a market for one business following a particular strategy, so one firm may be able to trade successfully on being the cheapest, while another will need to find a key point of differentiation if consumers are to recognise their product as offering any significant difference to its rivals.

> **Marketing strategy** is the term used to describe the general approach to marketing used by a business.

Choosing marketing strategies

REVISED ☐

Mass market strategies

A basic choice faced by a business is whether to attempt to sell a standard product to almost all consumers in a market – a mass market strategy – or whether to concentrate their efforts on selling specialised products to smaller subsections of the market – a niche market strategy.

Table 4.5 Benefits of mass market and niche market strategies

Benefits of successful mass market strategy	Benefits of successful niche market strategy
High distribution levels	Able to meet consumer needs more precisely
Greater control over advertising and promotion	Able to charge a higher price than mass market products
A degree of influence over pricing within the market	Less direct competition

Successful mass marketing probably relies on one major balancing act – the need to differentiate the product from all rivals without making it less appealing to any particular group of consumers. This can be a very tricky balance as many methods of product differentiation will reduce the appeal of the product to some groups of consumers. An example of this is differentiation through quality, excluding consumers unwilling to pay the associated higher price.

Niche market strategies

Although marketing to small subsections of the market is a fertile area for small specialist businesses to achieve success, some larger firms do use a niche marketing approach. Often the key to successful niche marketing is a depth of understanding of the product and consumer tastes that takes many years to build up. As a result, entering a niche market tends to be something that cannot be rushed – a patient approach is needed to ensure that consumers' needs are met appropriately.

Business to consumer (B2C) strategies

With business to consumer marketing, getting and keeping the right image for the product/service is vital. Of course, all aspects of the marketing mix contribute towards creating the image, so continually revisiting the marketing mix to ensure that consumers are getting the overall product they want is vital. The goal of any business to consumer marketing strategy must be developing customer loyalty among an ever growing base of customers.

Business to business (B2B) strategies

Business to business marketing is, of course, underpinned by the same principles as business to consumer marketing – that of developing customer loyalty. What differs tends to be the key characteristics of product or service that business customers are looking for. What is missing in business to business transactions is emotion, something that can often play a key role in business to consumer marketing. Instead, what matters most to business is price and reliability.

Figure 4.4 helps to summarise the key differences and shared end-goal of business to consumer and business to business marketing.

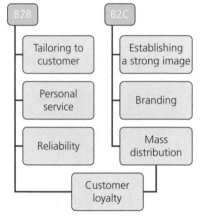

Figure 4.4 Logic chain: B2B v. B2C

Consumer behaviour – developing customer loyalty

REVISED

Customer loyalty can be thought of as being even deeper than simply generating repeat purchases. Really successful marketing does build some kind of emotional attachment between consumers and the brand. Critical here is ensuring not just that each aspect of the marketing mix is 'right', but also that the different aspects of the mix genuinely combine to create a clear image for the product. Then, if that image really is one that appeals to consumers in the market, that emotional bond can be created – the kind of bond that sees an almost religious devotion to products such as Apple electronics, Cadbury's Dairy Milk or BMW cars.

Now test yourself

TESTED

24 What are the three general characteristics of successful marketing strategy?
25 State two benefits of successful mass marketing.
26 State two benefits of successful niche marketing.
27 Briefly explain the reasons why successful business to business marketing differs from successful business to consumer marketing.

Answers on p. 123

Exam practice

A major multinational producer of household products has identified the following features of six of its major brands:

Product	Market share	Market growth
Brand A	High	High
Brand B	Low	High
Brand C	High	Low
Brand D	Low	High
Brand E	Low	High
Brand F	Low	Low

The company's marketing managers are devising their marketing strategy for the next three years and face a number of decisions.

Questions

1 Which brand is a cash cow? (2 marks)
2 What pricing strategies are most likely to have been used for the newly launched Brand E? (2 marks)
3 Using the Boston Matrix, advise the company on the strategies it might adopt in managing its portfolio over the next three years. (10 marks)

Answers and quick quiz 4 online

ONLINE

Summary

- Design can be a key tool in positioning a product within the market.
- Design involves balancing aesthetics, function and economy of manufacture.
- Good design brings a range of benefits to firms.
- In many businesses, design is influenced by environmental and ethical concerns.
- Different forms of promotion tend to have either a long- or a short-term impact.
- Promotions aimed at a short-term sales boost may damage brand image.
- Branding is a key form of product differentiation.
- Brands may be created for an individual product, for a range of products or for a whole business.
- Promotional methods that are effective at helping to build a brand include advertising, a USP, sponsorship or use of digital media.
- Recent developments in promotion and brand building have include viral marketing, use of social media and increased use of emotional branding.
- Pricing strategies set out the broad approach a firm will take to setting price.
- Two alternative strategies are available for firms launching new products: skimming and penetration.
- Four strategies (cost-plus, competitive, predatory and psychological) are used by firms selling existing products.

- The main factors determining the right pricing strategy all relate to the level of product differentiation (brand, competition, price elasticity).
- Other factors affecting the choice of pricing strategy include costs and the stage in the product life cycle.
- Distribution is crucial because it involves ensuring that consumers can buy the product where they want to buy it.
- Gaining distribution in retailers cannot be taken for granted.
- There are five main channels of distribution available to producers.
- Intermediaries can help spread products to a wider range of consumers but add to the final selling price of the product.
- The internet has opened significant opportunities in changing the way products are distributed.
- The product life cycle consists of four stages once the product has been launched.
- The stage of the product life cycle is likely to affect the marketing mix used for a product.
- New product development is often unsuccessful.
- Firms use the Boston Matrix to analyse their product portfolio.
- Mass marketing and niche marketing offer different benefits.
- Business to consumer and business to business marketing need to be addressed in different ways.

5 Managing people

Approaches to staffing

Staff as an asset vs staff as a cost

Some senior managers see the people that work for the firm as a source of potential competitive advantage. Others take a different approach, seeing staff as just another cost to be minimised. Key features of these approaches are shown in Table 5.1.

Table 5.1 Different ways of treating staff

Treating staff as an asset	Treating staff as a cost
Permanent contracts	Flexible contracts, perhaps **zero hours**
Develop staff skills with training	Minimal training offered
Pay staff a salary	Low pay, often at an hourly rate
Builds loyalty from staff	Often leads to a high **staff turnover** rate

Zero-hours contract is an employment contract that has a minimum of zero hours a week. So the employee is not guaranteed any work or income and is only told of their 'working week' a few days in advance.

Staff turnover is also called labour turnover and is the proportion of staff that leave a business during a year.

While it suits some businesses to keep their costs as low as possible, others will adopt a strategy of providing high-quality service which would encourage them to treat staff more as an asset to be nurtured and developed.

Flexible workforce

Flexibility refers to the ability of a business to adapt its operations to changes in patterns of demand. The way that staff are employed and managed can have a major impact on the flexibility of a business.

Why it is useful

A rapidly changing external environment means that patterns of demand can change rapidly, meaning that supply must change in response. Key drivers of these changes include:
- changes in the weather
- increased competition
- personalisation of products and services.

How to achieve it

There are a number of actions that a business can take to ensure that its human resources can be deployed as flexibly as necessary. Four key methods are explained below.

Multi-skilling

Using training to ensure that staff can perform a range of different roles within the business brings greater workforce flexibility. Instead of employing staff to perform just a single role, employees who are multi-skilled can cover for absent colleagues and also switch to roles that need to be filled when patterns in demand change.

Multi-skilling also tends to bring motivational benefits. Staff may enjoy the variety offered and may feel valued by the business as they receive greater training and skill development.

Part-time and temporary

Around a third of the UK's workforce are employed in part-time jobs. For some people, part-time hours allow them to fit work in alongside other commitments. This can help to bring people into the workplace who may offer excellent skills and experience but are unable to commit to full-time work. Temporary staff are employed on short-term contracts, meaning that if the employer no longer needs them, the contract is not renewed.

Flexible hours and home-working

For companies that treat their employees as an asset, staff may be allowed to choose when they work a set number of hours. Another way of increasing the flexibility of a job's requirements is to allow employees to work at home, or from home. This gives the staff greater flexibility to manage their time around other commitments. Developments in technology have made greater flexibility in location possible, with mobile phones and video messaging services such as Skype allowing face-to-face, immediate communication between people in different locations.

Flexibility for the employer may come from the use of zero-hours contracts. These are especially common in industries such as retailing and hospitality.

Outsourcing

Another method to increase capacity during times of high demand is to use other businesses to perform business functions. This is called **outsourcing**.

Benefits of outsourcing include:
● Ongoing fixed costs can be kept at a low level within the business.
● Sudden surges in demand can be met quickly.
● Companies to which work is outsourced can offer high-quality services.

Drawbacks of outsourcing:
● The company to which work is outsourced needs to make its own profit, adding to costs.
● Outsourcing arrangements may take time to work out.
● The company to which work is outsourced may not reach the required quality standards.

> **Outsourcing** means contracting another business to perform certain business functions, allowing significant increases in capacity when needed.

Dismissal vs redundancy

REVISED

Getting rid of staff can happen for a number of reasons, but these boil down to either a reduction in demand or incompetence or disruption from staff. In the first case, staff will be made redundant. Although making redundancies will reduce ongoing costs, the law requires businesses to compensate those made redundant according to how long they have worked for the business.

> **Exam tip**
>
> Although redundancies are an effective way of reducing costs in the long term, the need to make redundancy payments to staff means that in the short term there will be a significant cash outflow. This means that making redundancies is not a good way to resolve a cash flow problem.

Dismissal occurs either when an employee, having been fairly warned, is deemed 'not up to the job' or they have committed a major breach of their terms of employment – perhaps theft or some other dishonesty. In the case of an employee being fairly dismissed, no payments are made.

Employer/employee relations

There are times when an employer needs to discuss and agree certain changes with its entire workforce or at least groups of employees. This process of discussion and agreement is what is referred to when the term 'employer/employee relations' is used.

Collective bargaining

Collective bargaining occurs when an employer deals with one or a few representatives for the whole workforce when discussing problems, or negotiating pay rises or changes to working conditions. Most commonly, employees are represented by a trade union which will have a local representative who carries out bargaining with the employer on behalf of all the members. This approach is beneficial because:

● Employers only need to negotiate with one or two people on behalf of the whole workforce, thus saving time.
● Employees benefit because acting together gives them more power in their relationship with the employer.

Individual approach

This approach is, as its name suggests, the opposite of collective bargaining. It allows employees to be treated on an individual basis, with stars singled out for better treatment. However, it is far more time-consuming for the employer. Perhaps most importantly, the employer is in a stronger position if an employee is unable to call upon threats of strike action from their colleagues if they are unhappy with the deal being offered.

Now test yourself

TESTED

1 State three ways of creating a more flexible workforce.
2 What effect does redundancy have on the cash flow of a business?
3 What is the name given to the process of agreeing changes to pay and working conditions, with a trade union acting on behalf of its members?

Answers on p. 123

Recruitment, selection and training

Recruitment

The need to recruit could be triggered by:
● existing staff leaving
● growth of the business
● new activities needing new skills

This process allows a systematic approach to recruiting the right person to fill the vacancy, by carefully identifying what the vacant job involves and what skills will be required to do that job, and then attempting to attract a suitable number of applicants from which to choose.

Initially the recruitment process is designed to attract potential applicants. Then the selection part of the process begins in order to reduce the field of applicants to the best person for the job. The decision on whether to recruit **internally** or **externally** will depend on the:

- cost of the recruitment method
- size of the recruitment budget
- location and characteristics of the likely candidates.

Internal recruitment means filling a job vacancy with somebody who already works for the business.

External recruitment means filling a job vacancy with somebody who does not currently work for the business.

Table 5.2 Advantages and disadvantages of internal recruitment

Advantages of internal recruitment	Disadvantages of internal recruitment
Quicker and cheaper than external recruitment	Limits the number of potential applicants
Chance of promotion may help boost morale within a business that frequently recruits internally	Fails to bring in new ideas from outside the business
The skills and attitudes of internal candidates will already be known by the business	Creates a vacancy elsewhere in the business that will still need to be filled externally

Selection

REVISED

Once applications for a vacancy have been received, the business must now narrow down the field so that it is left with the best candidate for the vacancy. The selection process may require candidates to undergo a number of different procedures. The most common are outlined in Table 5.3.

Table 5.3 Common methods of selection for job vacancies

Method of selection	Explanation	Analysis
Interviews	Still the most common method, interviews can take place face to face or by telephone. They offer the chance to hold a conversation, allowing follow-up questions and some freedom of which areas to probe	Bias or prejudice on behalf of the interviewer may skew the results of interviews, undermining the usefulness of this method when used on its own
Testing and profiling	Attempting to bring objectivity to the selection process, aptitude tests can uncover just how high a candidate's skill levels are in certain tasks. Meanwhile, profiling helps to identify the personality-type of candidates	Purely objective selection methods can mean screening out great candidates who do not fit the 'traditional profile' of the job
Assessment centres	Candidates may be invited to attend an assessment centre where a range of selection methods from role plays to group tasks and interviews can be combined to better assess their abilities and performance in a simulated environment	This method tends to be more expensive than others and is more likely to be used only for more senior positions

Training

REVISED

Seen by Herzberg as the most powerful tool at a manager's disposal, **training** allows employees to develop new skills, thus boosting the range of tasks they are capable of performing.

The benefits and costs of training for a business are shown in Table 5.4.

Training is designed to enhance employees' existing skills or develop new skills.

Table 5.4 Benefits and costs of training for a business

Benefits	Costs
Higher skill levels can boost productivity and innovation	Providing training can carry a large financial cost
A wider range of skills can enhance the business's flexibility	While training is being provided, the normal operations of the business can be disrupted
Motivates staff who feel they have been invested in by the business	Better-trained staff are more attractive to other businesses which may try to poach them

On-the-job versus off-the-job training

Figure 5.1 shows the advantages and disadvantages of on-the-job training. Choosing to use off-the-job training prevents the two disadvantages but means the business can miss out on the advantages offered by on-the-job training.

> **Induction training** is the term that specifically describes initial training when an employee begins a job that is designed to familiarise them with the workplace and the business.

> **Typical mistake**
>
> Do not be tempted to use the term 'induction training' to describe all training that offers employees new skills. It relates only to the training provided at the beginning of a member of staff's employment.

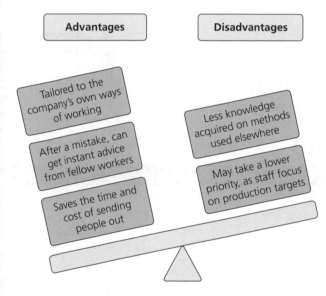

Figure 5.1 Advantages and disadvantages of on-the-job training

Now test yourself

TESTED

4 State two reasons why on-the-job training may be more effective than off-the-job training.
5 State two reasons why off-the-job training may be more effective than on-the-job training.
6 Why can interviews be an unreliable method of selection?
7 Give two benefits of internal recruitment.
8 Give two benefits of external recruitment.

Answers on p. 123

Organisational design

Structure

REVISED

As organisations begin to grow, thought must be given to the way in which the different people and jobs are to be structured. This helps in ensuring that the work is co-ordinated effectively and the organisation is following its correct strategic path. Most organisations have a hierarchical system, with the main decisions taken at the top and those lower down the structure putting those decisions into practice. These structures are usually split vertically into **business functions**.

Other aspects of traditional organisational structures include the need for each member of staff to have a single boss – a **line manager**. This helps to ensure that each employee knows whom to take orders from and to whom they must be answerable for any mistakes.

Each manager should not be expected to supervise too many members of staff, otherwise they would not be able to perform this role effectively. Therefore it is important to design an organisation where individual managers' **spans of control** are not too wide.

Limiting spans of control means that for larger organisations, many levels of hierarchy are needed. Therefore, management levels can run from functional managers (such as the marketing manager), through other senior management roles (brand manager), to regional managers, location managers and then supervisors and team leaders. At each layer, different levels of power and responsibility are found – the nearer the top, the more power and responsibility (and pay).

Vertical paths through the organisation, through which communication passes, are referred to as chains of command.

Subtle differences can be found between organisations, especially when relating to where key decisions are made. In a centralised organisational structure, to aid co-ordination, most significant decisions will be made at the very top of the structure. In other organisations, perhaps those where local conditions vary greatly, it makes more sense to allow local managers to make decisions for their branch. Figure 5.2 helps to explain the potential benefits of both centralised and decentralised decision-making.

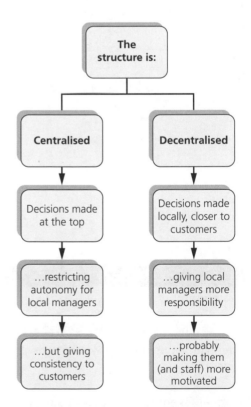

Figure 5.2 Centralised vs decentralised organisations

Business functions are the main departments working within a business. The traditional business functions are marketing, finance, human resource management and operations management.

A **line manager** is a single boss for each member of staff, from whom orders must be taken and to whom actions must be explained where necessary.

Span of control is the term used to describe the number of subordinates directly answerable to one manager.

Centralised structure describes an organisational structure where most major decisions are taken at the very top of the organisation by the most senior managers.

Decentralised structure is the opposite of a centralised structure and is where decision-making is passed lower down the organisation structure through the process of delegation.

Delegation means passing decision-making power down the organisational structure to a lower level.

Typical mistake

Delegation does not mean simply telling someone to do something – that is simply issuing orders. For delegation to take place, some actual decision-making power over how to do a job must be passed down to a subordinate.

Types of structure

REVISED

A further fundamental difference in organisational structure concerns the basic shape of the structure.

Tall

A tall structure is one with many layers and narrow spans of control. Table 5.5 summarises the advantages and disadvantages of a tall structure with narrow spans of control.

Table 5.5 Advantages and disadvantages of a tall structure with narrow spans of control

Advantages	Disadvantages
Allows close supervision of staff	Staff may feel over-supervised and not trusted by their management
Communication within the immediate team (boss and immediate subordinates) is likely to be excellent	Communications as a whole may be poor with so many layers for messages to pass through
Many layers of hierarchy means plenty of opportunities for promotion to the next level	With narrow spans, there may be little scope for staff to use their initiative

Flat

A flat structure has fewer levels within the hierarchy, but wider spans of control. This forces increased delegation by managers who are unable to closely supervise far higher numbers of subordinates. Of course, this can result in more mistakes. It can also lead to far greater motivation from staff, who are expected to use their own initiative. A flat structure also has the benefit of reducing the number of layers between the top of the structure and the very lowest level. This may make it easier for senior managers to develop an understanding of the real day-to-day challenges faced by staff dealing with customers, for example. This can increase the ability of the firm to respond to changes in customers' tastes, boosting competitiveness.

Matrix

A matrix structure differs from traditional structures in one very significant way. Instead of only having one line manager, staff may have two, or even more. Though a traditional functional structure is likely to exist, cross-functional project teams are formed, with staff from different departments working together on a project, under the leadership of the project leader.

Table 5.6 Advantages and disadvantages of a matrix structure

Advantages of a matrix structure	Disadvantages of a matrix structure
Working together allows expertise from each department to be immediately available, preventing possible delays in projects	Each project team member will have at least two bosses
The focus of the project team should be on success of the project, rather than making their functional department more important than others	Two bosses means it can be unclear whose orders should take priority
Learning from the views of colleagues in other departments helps to develop each team member	Getting staff from different functional areas to agree can be difficult

Impact of structure on motivation and efficiency

It is remarkable how many ways structure can affect efficiency and motivation and therefore costs and profit. Effects on efficiency and therefore unit costs include:
- poor communication leading to mistakes
- duplication of tasks
- tasks being overlooked and not done
- departments failing to work together effectively.

Meanwhile, structure can affect motivation by encouraging or preventing the following key issues:
- Scope to show initiative
- Extent of delegation
- Responsibility
- Receiving all information required to perform a job
- Opportunities for promotion

> **Exam tip**
>
> Whenever relevant, look to build chains of logic that interweave organisational structure, motivation theory, productivity (efficiency) and unit costs.

Now test yourself

9 In what type of structure may staff have more than one line manager?
10 Why does a flat structure encourage delegation?
11 How does a tall structure offer more scope for promotion?
12 Who makes major decisions in a centralised structure?
13 Look ahead to the next section which deals with motivation in theory. Link up each of the five bullet points above to the work of at least one theorist to understand how you can use motivation theory alongside organisational structure when building a chain of argument in an exam answer.

Answers on p. 123

Motivation in theory

The desire to understand what motivates people to work is driven by the commercial need to fully use the human resources at the firm's disposal. For over a century, academics have been trying to put together viable theories that help to explain what motivates people to work. The four key theorists are explained below.

F.W. Taylor (scientific management)

Frederick Winslow Taylor's approach to motivation can be summarised simply as 'money motivates'. His theory suggests that people only work in order to maximise their own income. This means that to get people to work harder, money should be used as an incentive (or removal of money as a threat). This approach to motivation was accompanied by Taylor's beliefs as to how work as a whole should be organised, summarised below:
- Observe workers at work.
- Identify the most efficient workers and how they do the job.
- Break the task down into small, simple repetitive parts.
- Devise equipment specifically designed to speed up the process.
- Set out clear-cut instructions for what each employee must do.
- Design a payment system that rewards each worker each time they complete their task.

F.W. Taylor's work is still visible in many jobs today, where commission or piece rate pay is used to incentivise more work being completed. However, Taylor's ideas of how a business should be organised became extremely unpopular with workers. They felt treated like pieces of machinery and denied the opportunity to use their minds at work. They were also resentful of the level of control that the work process and payment method gave employers.

Elton Mayo (human relations theory)

REVISED ☐

Mayo's work stemmed from a range of experiments he conducted into the effectiveness of 'Taylorism'. As he carried out more and more workplace-based experiments, Mayo discovered that there were more factors affecting workplace performance than money. Mayo's findings centred on the importance of interpersonal relations as a factor affecting productivity, thus the name 'human relations theory'. The factors Mayo identified are summarised below:

● Workers gain satisfaction from a certain level of freedom and control over their working environment.
● Workers who feel they belong to a team tend to work more effectively.
● Group norms (what people in a team expect of each other) tend to have a strong influence over workers' behaviour and productivity.
● Communication between workers and between managers and workers improves morale.
● Managers taking an active personal interest in their employees has a beneficial impact on workers' performance.

Maslow (hierarchy of needs)

REVISED ☐

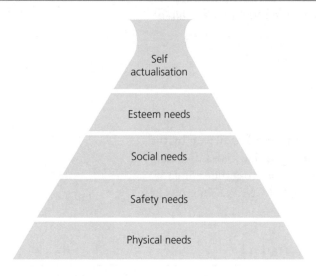

Figure 5.3 Maslow's hierarchy of needs

Abraham Maslow's hierarchy of needs, shown in Figure 5.3, summarises his beliefs about what explains human behaviour, both in general and in the workplace. He believed that all humans have five sets of needs. These can be arranged in a hierarchy, with the most basic needs for life at the bottom and the higher-level needs at the top. Meeting each level of needs is a priority until they are met, when a person will focus on the next unsatisfied level of needs. Businesses use the hierarchy to understand how to motivate their staff using a range of techniques. The hope is to move people up the hierarchy to the higher-level needs which tend to generate the best level of workplace performance. Table 5.7 shows how each level of need has workplace implications.

Table 5.7 Maslow's hierarchy of needs: implications for business

Maslow's level of human need	Business implications
Physical needs, e.g. food, shelter, warmth	Pay levels and working conditions
Safety needs, e.g. security, a safe structured environment, stability, freedom from anxiety	Job security, a clear job role/description, clear lines of accountability (only one boss)
Social needs, e.g. belonging, friendship, contact	Team working, communications, social facilities
Esteem needs, e.g. strength, self-respect, confidence, status and recognition	Status, recognition for achievement, power, trust
Self-actualisation, e.g. self-fulfilment; 'to become everything that one is capable of becoming', wrote Maslow	Scope to develop new skills and meet new challenges, and to develop one's full potential

Frederick Herzberg (two-factor theory)

REVISED

Herzberg's theory relies on accepting his definition of motivation – of doing something because you want to do it. He distinguished this from *movement*, which he defined as doing something to get a reward or avoid a punishment. Herzberg was clear – motivated workers give you their best performance all the time, are willing to embrace change and are great at solving problems. Workers who do things to gain rewards or avoid threats will only do so while the reward is available or the threat remains. Even worse, they are likely to get stuck into a single way of doing things and therefore resist change.

Professor Herzberg's two-factor theory suggests that factors affecting people at work can be grouped into 'motivators' and 'hygiene factors'. He identifies five common features of instances when workers are genuinely motivated. Providing the opportunity for staff to experience these can lead to job satisfaction. Herzberg's motivators are:
- achievement
- recognition for achievement
- meaningful, interesting work
- responsibility
- advancement – a sense of growth as a person.

All of these needs relate to the work you actually ask an employee to do. The other set of needs all relate to the context, or environment, in which you expect an employee to do their job. These needs, which Herzberg called hygiene factors, must be met to prevent an employee feeling dissatisfied.
- Company policy and administration (the rules and paperwork involved in working for the business)
- Supervision
- Pay
- Interpersonal relations (with peers, bosses or subordinates)
- Working conditions

These hygiene needs do not motivate staff, however they must be satisfied to prevent dissatisfaction. Herzberg argued it is impossible to motivate a dissatisfied worker. Three possible scenarios are explained in Table 5.8.

> **Typical mistake**
>
> Suggesting that Herzberg claimed that pay and bonuses motivate staff is wrong. Herzberg was clear that money is a hygiene factor and while offering bonuses can generate movement (better than average work), it does not motivate.

> Herzberg used the term **job enrichment** to describe designing jobs that include the motivators. Possible methods include: a complete unit of work, direct feedback on performance and the ability to communicate directly with any other member of staff.

Table 5.8 Three scenarios under Herzberg's two-factor theory

Hygiene needs met, no motivators	Worker will give movement (not their best – only enough to gain reward or avoid threat)
Motivators met, but hygiene not satisfied	Employee will be resentful of their job and, no matter how interesting the work is, will perform poorly – and look for another job
Hygiene needs and motivators met	Employees can focus on their job and will do it to the best of their ability

Now test yourself

TESTED ☐

14 Explain how Taylor's belief in why people work ties in with paying people for each unit they produce.
15 Explain how this means a firm should be able to pay staff and make a profit.
16 What did Taylor say was the only thing that motivated people to work?
17 What did Mayo discover also played a part in motivation?
18 List Maslow's five levels of needs.
19 State two examples of Herzberg's hygiene factors and three of his motivators.
20 Explain in your own words the difference between motivation and movement, giving an example from your school/college life.

Answers on pp. 123–4

Motivation in practice

Financial rewards

REVISED ☐

- Piecework: Paying each member of staff a set amount of money each time they repeat a task.
  - Advantage: This encourages speed as the quickest staff earn the most money.
  - Disadvantage: It is likely to lead to quality problems as staff rush to complete as many tasks as possible.
- Commission: Paying staff whose role involves selling a certain percentage of the revenue they generate, usually on top of a low basic salary or hourly rate.
  - Advantage: This incentivises staff to sell as much as they can.
  - Disadvantage: It may lead to mis-selling as staff try to sell more expensive products or services to maximise their commission, causing customer dissatisfaction.
- Bonus: Paying a lump sum as an additional reward to members of staff, typically once a year.
  - Advantage: This can provide an excellent way of offering staff a valued extra thank you.
  - Disadvantage: Large bonuses can distort staff behaviour, emphasising the need to reach the bonus target by whatever means possible.
- Profit-sharing: Allocating a certain proportion of annual profits to be shared as a bonus among staff.
  - Advantage: This aligns staff goals with business goals.
  - Disadvantage: Hard-working staff may resent others who receive the same profit share bonus without putting in the same amount of effort.

- Performance-related pay (PRP): This involves rewarding staff whose performance exceeds a certain level where work performance is hard to quantify. The decision whether to award a bonus usually depends on some form of appraisal system.
  - Advantage: This allows individuals' performances to be clearly rewarded financially.
  - Disadvantage: Employees may feel the process used to decide on the award of PRP is unfair or biased against them.

Non-financial techniques

REVISED

> **Delegation** means passing authority down the structure to a subordinate, giving them some decision-making power over how a task is done.
>
> **Empowerment** is a slightly stronger form of delegation in which the subordinate is given some decision-making power over what tasks need to be done, not simply told how to do them.
>
> **Consultation** means asking the views of staff affected as part of a decision-making process, although the manager retains the power to make the decision.
>
> **Job enlargement** is the term used to describe any increase in the scope of a job and this describes both job rotation and job enrichment.

Table 5.9 Non-financial motivation techniques

	Explanation	Why it should motivate	Possible problems
Delegation	Passing decision-making power to staff over how to perform a task	Allows staff to meet Maslow's esteem and self-actualisation needs, as well as being a motivator for Herzberg	Staff must have the skills and experience to make good decisions
Empowerment	Passing even more power to staff, to the extent where they may be given authority to decide what job needs doing	Allows staff to meet Maslow's esteem and self-actualisation needs, as well as being a motivator for Herzberg	The need for appropriate skills and experience is even greater than that needed for successful delegation
Consultation	Seeking staff's opinions before making a decision	May help to meet esteem needs on Maslow's hierarchy	Many decisions will appear to go against the views of many staff – consultation may be seen as a meaningless process
Team-working	Allowing staff to work in a group rather than individually	Allows staff to meet Maslow's social needs, recognises Mayo's belief that human relations are necessary to motivate staff	The performance of more productive individuals may be dragged down to a team average level
Flexible working	Allows staff to adjust where and/or when they work to suit their lifestyle	Helps to ensure Maslow's lower-level needs are met, and can be a key factor in meeting Herzberg's hygiene needs	Co-ordinating the workforce can be harder to achieve
Job enrichment	Giving staff added responsibilities and challenge by widening the scope of their job	Meets Herzberg's motivators and Maslow's top two levels of need	Some staff may view extra responsibility as an unwanted burden
Job rotation	Moves staff between different tasks of the same level of complexity	Helps to prevent boredom – little theoretical justification	Prevents the potential productivity benefits that come from specialising in one task

Now test yourself

TESTED

21 State three motivation methods that F.W. Taylor would advocate.
22 State three motivation methods that Herzberg would advise a business to use.
23 What motivation method could be used if workers are struggling to meet their social needs at work?
24 Explain why delegation may need to be accompanied by training.
25 Which motivation methods are designed to align a worker's personal financial rewards with the company's financial success?

Answers on p. 124

Leadership

Leaders and managers

REVISED

The roles of **manager** and **leader** are different, although in many businesses, especially smaller firms, the same person may be expected to fulfil both roles. Peter Drucker's quotation 'Managers do things right; leaders do the right thing' sums up the difference nicely.

A **manager** is a person fulfilling a role whose major job is to oversee putting plans into action, getting the details right and ensuring that the resources allocated are used correctly.

The role of a **leader** is to identify key issues to be addressed, set objectives and decide what should be done to address those issues and who should do it.

Table 5.10 Responses of leaders and managers to different circumstances

Circumstances	What managers do	What leaders do
Key staff are leaving	Recruit new staff with care	Rethink the design and responsibilities within the job
An important customer is threatening to go elsewhere	Get staff to smooth things over as best they can	Take personal responsibility for the customer's disappointment and sort the problem out
A downturn means redundancies are necessary	Hire an HR specialist company to handle the whole process	Call a staff meeting, explain what is happening and deal with the whole thing personally
A very promising new product idea has been proposed	Take control of the development and assemble a large project team	Delegate the project to a bright young manager, providing extra resources when needed

Typical mistake

Although some leaders are charismatic characters, with outgoing personalities that subordinates love to follow, many highly successful leaders may go unnoticed – not all great leaders lead by example.

Types of leadership style

REVISED

Different leaders deal with their staff in different ways. You need to understand four types of leadership style:

● Autocratic: Autocratic leaders issue instructions and expect these to be obeyed. They know exactly what they want done and pay little attention to what workers have to say. Communication will be one-way, top down, with the manager not expecting or responding to feedback.

- Paternalistic: Paternalistic leaders see themselves in the role of a traditional father-figure – the head of the family. They care about the best interests of staff/family and listen to their views. But the leader makes the decisions, albeit decisions believed to be in the best interests of staff.
- Democratic: Democratic managers expect their staff to be involved in decision-making. They will delegate authority to subordinates, believing that this is the best way to get the job done. Some democratic managers will agree clear objectives with staff, then let them get on with doing the job in order to achieve the objectives.
- Laissez-faire: Literally meaning 'leave to do', laissez-faire managers leave staff alone to get on with things, generally without even providing a clear sense of direction. This will often be the result of the manager being either too busy or too lazy to provide focus and structure. However, for a new business needing ideas and creativity, leaving talented creative staff alone can provide a fertile ground for innovation.

Table 5.11 Assumptions and approaches of three types of leader

	Democratic	Paternalistic	Autocratic
Style derived from	Belief in Maslow's higher-order needs or in Herzberg's motivators	Mayo's work on human relations and Maslow's lower- and middle-order needs	A Taylorite view of staff
Approach to staff	Delegation of authority	Consultation with staff	Orders must be obeyed
Approach to staff remuneration	Salary, perhaps plus employee shareholdings	Salary plus extensive fringe benefits	Payment by results, e.g. piece rate
Approach to human resource management	Recruitment and training based on attitudes and teamwork	Emphasis on training and appraisal for personal development	Recruitment and training based on skills; appraisal linked to pay

Now test yourself

TESTED ☐

26 Name the leadership style being explained:
   (a) The leader seeks and listens to the views of staff, delegating with a clear sense of purpose.
   (b) The manager cares about the welfare of staff and considers this when making decisions.
   (c) The manager expects their instructions to be followed and keeps all decision-making power.
   (d) The manager leaves staff to get on with their work without any clear direction.
27 Explain why the leader and manager are likely to be the same person in a small business.

Answers on p. 124

Exam practice

HMRC – the UK organisation responsible for collecting taxes – attracted news headlines in 2016 as a result of its decision to outsource the cleaning of its offices. This meant that cleaners, formerly employed by HMRC, might lose their pension benefits and legal entitlement to sick pay. The company to which the cleaning work was outsourced used staff employed on zero-hours contracts. This shifted the risk involved in employing staff away from HMRC to the subcontractor. In turn, the subcontractor shifts risk to the people they employ. The zero-hours contracts mean the subcontractor does not have to pay staff when there's no work, therefore avoiding unnecessary costs.

Questions

1 What is meant by a zero-hours contract? (2)
2 What is meant by outsourcing? (2)
3 Using a motivation theory of your choice, explain why HMRC's new cleaners, employed by the subcontractor, are likely to do a poorer job than cleaners who were previously employed by HMRC. (6)
4 Assess whether HMRC has made the right decision about how to have its offices cleaned. (10)

Answers and quick quiz 5 online

ONLINE

Summary

- Different employers may view their staff either as a critical asset to the business's success or simply as a cost to be minimised.
- Having a flexible workforce makes it easier to run a business successfully.
- Employer/employee relations can be based on either collective or individual bargaining.
- The need to recruit staff could be triggered by existing staff leaving, growth of the business, or new activities being performed by the business.
- Staff may be recruited internally or externally.
- Selection methods including interviews, testing and profiling, and assessment centres are used to decide which applicants to employ.
- Training staff has both benefits and costs.
- Initial training is called induction training.
- Training can be carried out on the job or off the job.
- Organisational structures can be classified as tall, flat or matrix.
- Key issues affecting the shape of organisational structure are spans of control and levels of hierarchy.

- Organisational structure can have major impacts on efficiency and motivation.
- Methods of motivating staff can fall into two categories: financial and non-financial methods.
- The five financial methods are: piecework, commission, bonus, profit-sharing and performance-related pay.
- Non-financial methods are: delegation, empowerment, consultation, team-working, flexible working, job rotation and job enrichment.
- Clear links can be drawn from the motivation theorists' work to explain why these methods should work.
- The roles of leader and manager are significantly different.
- Different leaders treat their staff in different ways. This is called their leadership style.
- The main leadership styles to focus on are: autocratic, paternalistic, democratic and laissez-faire.

6 Entrepreneurs and leaders

Role of an entrepreneur

Businesses could not exist without entrepreneurs. They are the individuals who spot business opportunities and then act in order to exploit the opportunity. Entrepreneurs must fulfil a number of roles within their businesses, as outlined below.

Creating and setting up a business

Generating a business idea

At the very heart of any entrepreneur's success is a good idea, probably based on an understanding of consumers. The main sources of business ideas are:

- Observation: Watching what other businesses are doing or how consumers behave may give an idea that can be copied elsewhere. Or it may suggest an idea that can be adjusted to work even more successfully.
- Brain-storming: This is the process of simply listing possible ideas without any selection involved; this will come later.
- Thinking ahead: This is spotting trends that will lead to changes in the future that will offer business opportunities, for example noting a government initiative to boost the number of apprenticeships and setting up a website specialising in advertising apprenticeships.
- Personal or business experience: Noticing that certain needs are not met through personal experience or within a workplace.
- Innovations: Scientific breakthroughs or major overhauls of an existing type of product may generate viable business ideas.

Spotting an opportunity

An idea will only become a viable business if a market exists for it. The ability to identify chances to turn ideas into saleable products or services relies on spotting an opportunity. Typical sources of opportunity tend to be centred on changes occurring in the wider world:

- Changes in technology: Increased computing power in mobile handsets broadens the range of possible apps that could be produced to meet a need for consumers to control something on the move.
- Changes in society: Trends in the way people behave, such as increased part-time work opportunities for the semi-retired, can represent an opportunity, such as a recruitment agency for retired workers.
- Changes in the economy: Differing rates of national or regional economic growth may offer opportunities to be exploited.
- Changes in the housing market: New housing developments may bring associated opportunities to service providers if local populations grow, or become wealthier.
- Or the use of one of the techniques outlined below to examine the market: market research or market mapping.

Market research

Entrepreneurs are likely to have to conduct any market research on a very small budget. Small, low-cost studies can still help, though. They may throw up an important opportunity.

Cheap market research methods could include:
- Walking around a local town: This will give the opportunity to see if there are any obvious gaps (what, no Thai restaurant?) in addition to being able to see which types of business seem to be most popular with locals.
- Spending time with other entrepreneurs: Entrepreneurs in other parts of the country may be willing to share their insights and experience, helping to boost an entrepreneur's understanding of consumers' behaviour.
- Discussions with friends: This could be dangerous as friends may not want to dampen an entrepreneur's enthusiasm; but they can act as a focus group that could throw up new insights.
- Producing a market map, as detailed on page 14.

Running and expanding a business

REVISED

There are four key habits that successful entrepreneurs commonly demonstrate in the way they run their businesses:
- They measure performance in an unbiased way: If there are problems these must be identified rather than ignored.
- They have an eye for detail: It is unlikely that anybody other than the entrepreneur will be as worried about getting the little things right.
- They have the ability to step back from the day-to-day issues: Only by thinking strategically will a new business be able to secure a long-term future.
- They love what they are doing: Without this, the motivation needed to do the three things above will drain away.

Some businesses are not suited to expansion as the idea and opportunities remain small-scale or localised. For other entrepreneurs, expansion may be vital to prevent others from developing an idea more successfully. The three major problems to avoid as an entrepreneur considering expansion are:
- Over-estimating demand: What works in one place may not work elsewhere.
- Failing to raise sufficient finance: It is a lack of cash that ultimately leads to all business failure. Without having made sure that the business has enough finance to support operating on a larger scale, the danger of running out of cash becomes acute.
- Not recruiting enough or the right people: As entrepreneurs expand their business they will find their limited time more stretched, with more to oversee (perhaps causing too much stress). It is therefore vital that when they recruit they get the right staff who understand the business philosophy and have the skills needed.

Innovation within a business

REVISED

If entrepreneurs are loosely defined as those who are able to generate and develop new business ideas, then there is a role for them even in large firms. The kind of creative and disruptive thinking that entrepreneurs can draw on is increasingly being sought by large businesses. They want to nurture innovation within their businesses as a way of maintaining a competitive advantage. Entrepreneurial behaviour within the setting of a large business – **intrapreneurship** – can be seen in many successful large businesses such as Facebook.

> **Intrapreneurship** is the name given to the encouragement of entrepreneurial behaviour within larger businesses.

Barriers to entrepreneurship

Funding

Following the financial crash of the last decade, banks in the UK have been less willing to lend to small firms and business start-ups, considering them relatively high risk for relatively low return as they are often believed to be relatively unprofitable. Without institutions willing to lend, entrepreneurship may die back in the UK.

Gender bias

UK entrepreneurs are three times as likely to be male as female. This statistical mismatch between the population/market and the people starting new businesses is likely to mean that much entrepreneurial talent in the UK is going to waste.

Lack of public sector support

Although the image of the entrepreneur has improved significantly in the UK over the past twenty years, some who work in the public sector view entrepreneurs sceptically, suspecting tax avoidance or motives based on greed. This perception in the public sector may lead to an education system that fails to value entrepreneurial skills or other barriers to entrepreneurship.

Anticipating risk and uncertainty in the business environment

Risk and uncertainty characterise the business environment for many firms. This is because of the wide number of external variables that the business cannot control, and may not even be able to influence. The role of the entrepreneur must include understanding the ways that uncertainty affects the business. In some cases the main cause of uncertainty can be reduced, such as introducing new products into the firm's portfolio, thereby reducing the dependence on the sales of one brand.

Now test yourself

1 State two ways that walking around the local town may help to identify a business opportunity.
2 Explain why entrepreneurs may find it harder to secure funding from banks than fifteen years ago.
3 What four habits are important for any entrepreneur to develop if they want to successfully start up their business?

Answers on p. 124

Entrepreneurial motives and characteristics

Characteristics and skills

The main characteristics required to become a successful entrepreneur are:

● understanding the market
● determination

- passion
- resilience
- the ability to cope with risk.

Taking sensible risks involves weighing up the risk and rewards that a course of action offers. Risk consists of the likelihood of things going wrong and the size of the consequences of things going wrong. Good entrepreneurs accept risk but will not take on any risk they consider to be too great.

Good entrepreneurs will need to be able to demonstrate a range of common skills:

- Financial skills: This involves understanding key financial documents and, more fundamentally, how finance allows a business to function.
- Persuasive abilities: Good entrepreneurs find a way of persuading many people to do many things that their business needs, from suppliers to staff to customers.
- Problem-solving skills: These are frequently shown by the ability to identify causes of the problem and solve the problem by addressing these causes.
- Networking skills: With a wide range of possible business contacts, entrepreneurs are more likely to find someone who can help when the business needs help.

Reasons why people set up businesses

REVISED

- Profit maximising: This means to continually seek to get the most profit from every business transaction. Though this may seem the way to get rich, it will often cause long-term problems, with consumers feeling exploited or even cheated with substandard work caused by skimping on materials and workmanship.
- **Profit satisficing**: Long-term success may well be based on satisficing, with the need to accept lower than possible profits in the short term to build a brand or a reputation.
- Independence: Entrepreneurs sometimes set up their own business to avoid the need to take orders from others or fit in with company policy. Research shows the attractions of 'being your own boss' to be a very common motive.
- Home-working: Being able to work at, or from, home can be another form of independence, especially valued by those with family commitments.
- Ethical stance: For those with strong beliefs in how business should be done, their ethical stance may lead them to feel the need to start their own business. They are unwilling to compromise their beliefs by working in a business with whose practices they feel uncomfortable.
- Social entrepreneurship: Although this has a clear cross-over with ethical beliefs, some entrepreneurs will start up a business whose major aim is to make a positive contribution to their community, perhaps by providing a service that benefits people in need. Sadly, some may pretend to be social entrepreneurs while profit remains their real goal.

> **Profit satisficing** means blending a desire for profit with other factors, such as building a good reputation or having a good work–life balance.

> **Exam tip**
>
> An entrepreneur's motives will be a major determining factor behind their decision-making. Decisions taken by an entrepreneur who is seeking to maximise profit will differ greatly from those taken by an entrepreneur driven by an ethical stance.

Now test yourself

TESTED

4 What are two common financial motives for starting a business?
5 Briefly explain a good entrepreneur's attitude to risk.
6 State three types of people on whom an entrepreneur may need to use their persuasive abilities.
7 Why can profit maximisation damage a firm's long-term chances of success?
8 Why may entrepreneurs who take an ethical stance struggle to make a profit, even in the long term?

Answers on p. 124

Business objectives

Business **objectives** are targets set in order to ensure that the whole business is working towards the same goals. Objectives are set by those in charge of the firm, such as the chief executive. Once objectives have been set, a plan for achieving the objectives – a **strategy** – can be devised. The strategy will lay out what each department of the business will need to do in order to enable the business to reach its objectives.

An **objective** is a specific target set by a business.

The **strategy** is the plan devised by the business to achieve its objectives.

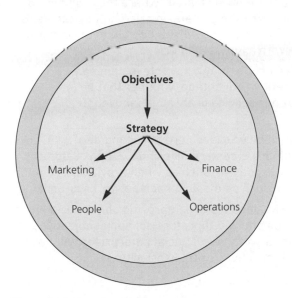

Figure 6.1 How business works

SMART objectives

REVISED

To gain most from objectives, they should be SMART:
● Specific
● Measurable
● Achievable
● Realistic
● Time-bound

Common business objectives

REVISED

Common business objectives can be seen in Table 6.1.

Table 6.1 Common business objectives

Typical objective	Explanation	Typical circumstances
Survival	Focusing on generating sufficient cash to sustain the business	When starting up, or when a challenging external environment threatens the future of the business, such as a recession or the arrival of a powerful new competitor
Profit maximisation	Earning the most profit possible in a given time period	A common objective for businesses – reflecting the need to generate profit for owners as a primary purpose of business
Sales maximisation	Growing the number of customers, without a major focus on controlling costs	In a rapidly growing market, firms may try to maximise their share of the market, with an expectation of generating profits once the market growth has slowed and competition reduces

Typical objective	Explanation	Typical circumstances
Market share	Increasing market share to a dominant level helps to ensure long-term success through greater distribution and preventing new entrants from challenging in the market	Market leaders will often seek to increase their lead and thus power by enhancing market share
Cost efficiency	A focus on seeking to minimise the costs of producing a product or service and the running costs of the business	This objective will be key for firms that are trying to follow a strategy where they will aim to undercut all their rivals on price. If they can keep costs low, they should still be able to make a profit even with a low selling price
Employee welfare	Looking after staff, by treating them well, and looking to develop them using training and internal recruitment	Where people play a key role in gaining a competitive advantage, whether that be in customer service or through innovation
Customer satisfaction	Prioritising the need to ensure that every customer has a positive interaction with the business	This will be crucial where attracting new customers is costly and losing existing customers is very expensive, such as when providing a regular service such as mobile phone networks or banking
Social objectives	Objectives that relate to the beneficial role a business can play within society	Some businesses see improving society as a key purpose and will therefore set social objectives in a meaningful way. Social enterprises will have social objectives as a top priority

Exam tip

Successful firms choose the right objectives to suit their circumstances. Carefully read the right-hand column of Table 6.1 to ensure you understand when different objectives are most appropriate.

Now test yourself

TESTED ☐

9 Why do businesses set objectives?
10 What does SMART stand for?
11 What are the eight common business objectives?

Answers on p. 124

Forms of business

The topic referred to as 'forms of business' refers primarily to the legal status of the organisation. However, later in this topic, 'Other forms of business' covers issues such as licensing the use of a business's name, running a business enterprise to improve society, running a business as part of a lifestyle choice and running a business purely online.

Table 6.2 Different forms of business

Legal forms of business covered in this topic	Other 'forms of business' covered – not specifically relating to legal status
Sole trader	Franchising
Partnership	Social enterprise
Private limited company	Lifestyle businesses
Public limited company	Online businesses

Exam practice answers and quick quizzes at **www.hoddereducation.co.uk/myrevisionnotes**

Businesses with unlimited liability

REVISED

Sole trader

A sole trader is a person who starts and runs a business without turning it into a company. This explains why the law sees the business and the owner of the business as the same. As a result, the owner is personally **liable** for any debts built up in running their business. If the business goes bust, the owner has to use personal assets to repay those to whom the business owes money.

> **Liability** refers to the extent to which the owner(s) of the business must repay debts incurred in the running of the business.

Key benefits:
- Owner has full control over decisions
- Owner keeps all profits made
- Minimal paperwork needed to start up

Key drawbacks:
- Owner has unlimited liability for debts
- Hard to raise finance

Partnership

While a sole trader is the single owner of a business, a partnership is perhaps best thought of as a sole trader where several owners are allowed. This helps to raise finance as each partner can bring capital into the business. In addition, the burden of responsibility for running the business can be shared, potentially among people with varied skills and experience. As with a sole trader, partners still have **unlimited liability** for debts incurred in running the business.

> **Typical mistake**
>
> Sole traders can employ staff. Too many exam answers wrongly state that a sole trader has to run the business by themselves, mistakenly believing sole traders are literally one-person businesses. The 'sole' refers to the owner – just one owner. There can be as many staff employed as the owner wishes.

Key benefits:
- More owners can allow more finance to be raised
- Partners may bring varied skills and experience
- Shared burden of responsibility among partners

Key drawbacks:
- Partners have unlimited liability
- Potential for disagreement among partners

> **Unlimited liability** means that the owners of the business must take personal responsibility for covering debts run up by their business. If the business goes bust, the owner can be forced to sell their own personal assets to repay lenders, suppliers or employees to whom money is owed.

> **Typical mistake**
>
> Liability for debt only becomes an issue if the business goes bust. The owners' personal assets will only be taken if the business goes under, but still owes money after the assets bought for use in the business have been sold to raise money.

Businesses with limited liability

REVISED

For businesses happy to undergo increased legal formalities, **limited liability** for owners offers a great safety net from which to build a much larger business. Without this protection, far fewer investors would be willing to invest their money into multi-billion pound firms whose debts could run into billions of pounds.

> **Limited liability** is a form of legal protection for business owners which ensures that owners of a limited company can only lose the money they have invested in the business.

Private limited company

The simpler form of limited company to start is a private limited company with no minimum share capital. Increased legal formalities include having accounts independently audited each year at a probable cost of several thousand pounds.

Public limited company

A public limited company is the only type of business that can sell shares via the stock market to the general public. This allows them to raise vast sums of share capital. However, in order to become a public limited company, a business must have a minimum of £50,000 share capital. In addition, there are considerable regulatory requirements involved in floating the company on the stock market. Continuing to meet the annual requirements of the stock market will cost tens or hundreds of times more than running a private limited company.

Other forms of business

REVISED

Franchising

Franchising offers the opportunity to start a business using a tried and tested formula. For the **franchisor**, franchising can be a relatively cheap and quick way of expanding their business rapidly. For the **franchisee**, there are both benefits and drawbacks relative to starting entirely independently, as shown below.

Benefits:
- Access to a tried and tested formula for business success
- Support from the franchisor in providing materials and fixtures and fittings
- Advice and training on all business functions
- Possibility of a national advertising campaign from the franchisor
- A guaranteed local monopoly for that brand
- Easier access to loans as banks recognise the lower risk involved in starting as a franchisee

Drawbacks:
- The franchisee may feel frustrated at being unable to make decisions dictated by the franchisor.
- There is likely to be an initial franchise fee to buy the licence (perhaps several hundred thousand pounds for the most popular franchised brands).
- The franchisor will also expect royalties, a percentage of revenue.

A **franchise** is a licence to use another business's name and business model in return for payment.

A **franchisor** is a business that sells the right to use its name and logo to other businesses or entrepreneurs.

A **franchisee** is an entrepreneur or company that buys a licence to use another business's name and business model in return for payment.

Social enterprise

Social enterprises place the desire to fix a social problem above the profit motive when making decisions. This is, of course, a terribly broad definition but that is necessary given the wide range of businesses that can be classed as being, in some way, social enterprises.

Lifestyle businesses

Some entrepreneurs start up a business because it suits their desired lifestyle. This may mean that maximising profit is far from the most important issue considered when making decisions for these businesses. For some, running their own business may give flexibility in working hours to fit around family commitments: for example, leaving a highly paid job that requires long periods away from home in order to start up a small computer repair business could allow an entrepreneur to fit work commitments round their children's sports days and Christmas plays.

Other lifestyle businesses may be based around hobbies or pastimes. Starting up a football coaching business can offer an entrepreneur the chance to spend not just their spare time but also their work time on a football pitch, doing the thing they love. In such cases, maximising profit may be less important than simply making enough money to sustain the lifestyle.

Online businesses

As the internet has grown over the past 30 years to become a huge part of modern life, business opportunities have grown out of the technology. Most important is the way the internet has enabled businesses to connect with consumers effectively without the need to ever meet face to face. The result is that traditional 'bricks and mortar' businesses now face competition from many online-only companies. In general, online offers two powerful advantages over traditional 'bricks and mortar' businesses:

- Lower costs (with no need to spend on physical premises)
- Higher potential revenues (with the scope to sell worldwide)

Now test yourself
TESTED

12 Which two types of business organisation offer their owners no limited liability?
13 What is the minimum share capital required to form a public limited company?
14 State two benefits of starting a business by buying a franchise.
15 State two drawbacks of buying a franchise rather than starting a business independently.

Answers on pp. 124–5

Business choices

Rather than worrying about learning too much in this topic, being aware of **opportunity cost**, choices and trade-offs should help to structure the thought processes needed to write excellent responses to examination questions.

> **Opportunity cost** is the value of the next best option forgone when a business decision is made.

Opportunity cost
REVISED

Too often business decisions are made without a real appreciation of the opportunity cost. In order to genuinely understand the opportunity cost of any decision, it is vital to ensure that all possible options are appropriately quantified. However, this generally needs accurate forecasting, a challenge that most businesses struggle to achieve.

Frequently, decisions may be based on personal preferences of business leaders – leaders in a position to influence the data on which the decision will be made. Though this may sound conspiratorial, it may in fact simply be a reflection of the enthusiasm that the leader has for their 'great idea'. If the best decisions are to be made, cool heads must carefully identify the opportunity costs involved in making a particular business choice.

Identifying opportunity costs requires careful thought and analysis. Figure 6.2 helps to illustrate this.

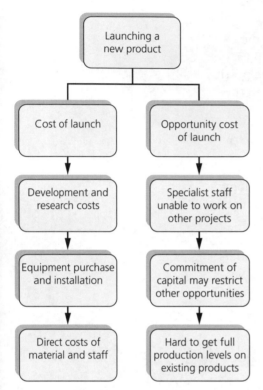

Figure 6.2 Opportunity costs of new product launch

Choices and trade-offs

The choices a business faces are likely to involve some form of compromise – a trade-off between competing objectives – such as minimising costs and maintaining quality standards. Successfully managing these trade-offs will need several attributes on behalf of decision-makers including:

● experience
● understanding of consumer tastes
● a broad understanding of the business's current position
● an understanding of the external issues influencing the decision.

Now test yourself

16 Explain the meaning of the term 'opportunity cost'.
17 Explain the meaning of the term 'trade-off'.

Answers on p. 125

Moving from entrepreneur to leader

Once a business start-up has been successful, for those entrepreneurs who are happy to grow their business a number of problems may emerge. Some of these issues will be caused by changes within the business. One of the most common, though, is the challenge for the founder in making the transition from entrepreneur to leader.

Table 6.3 Common issues when moving from entrepreneur to leader

Common business issues	Common personal issues
Matching production to demand	Delegating
Financing growth	Maintaining effective communication
Overtrading	Co-ordinating far more people
Change in structure	Keeping an eye on the big issues

Business issues

REVISED

Matching production to demand

In order for growth to take place, the business must stimulate more demand. This is likely to be achieved by targeting new markets, perhaps by opening a new branch in a different town or by launching new variations of the original product to suit different tastes. In each scenario, the business will need to attempt to forecast demand in a less familiar market than the one in which it has been operating thus far.

An overly optimistic forecast will result in too much cash tied up in stock causing significant cash flow problems. Underestimate demand and the expansion can be doomed to failure if first-time customers arrive to find empty shelves or products unavailable.

Financing growth

In order to expand, output will need to increase and this is likely to require extra cash in order to finance increased materials, wages and possibly rental or purchase of new property or facilities. The challenge for a new business is to find a way of raising extra finance that avoids giving away too much of the business or excessive costs of finance. Note the common methods of financing growth along with the associated drawbacks:

- Sell shares: This will result in loss of control for entrepreneur.
- Loans: Interest and repayments will drain cash from the business and security may be required.
- Overdraft: Interest rates are even higher than on loans.
- Leasing new equipment: This will lead to higher costs in the long term as leasing fees will need to be paid for as long as the equipment is in use.

Ideally, retained profits can be used as a source of finance, but this source will not be available until the business has actually made a profit in the first place.

> **Typical mistake**
>
> Retained profits can only be used once as a source of finance. For example, if retained profit has already been spent on buying new equipment, that money is gone. It is also important to remember that not all profit is retained in a business – with interest and tax to pay and shareholders usually expecting to receive a dividend, businesses may not retain much of their operating profits.

Overtrading

The risk of **overtrading** is all too real for any business that expands rapidly. Figure 6.3 shows how overtrading can occur.

> **Overtrading** occurs when a firm expands too rapidly for its capital to cope with.

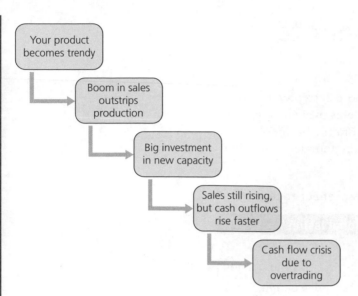

Figure 6.3 How overtrading happens

Overtrading illustrates why it is so important to ensure that growth is appropriately financed.

Change in structure

With more staff being taken on, extra layers are likely to need to be added to what may previously have been simply a two-level hierarchy, featuring the entrepreneur as boss and all other staff one level below the boss. To avoid the span of control getting too wide, managers or supervisors will now be required, but adding layers to the organisational structure fundamentally changes the way a business works. Much of the change relates to personal issues faced by the entrepreneur as their role shifts.

Personal issues

Successful entrepreneurs are often successful because they leave nothing to chance and rely on checking everything themselves. As a business grows, a single boss will eventually reach a point where they cannot check absolutely everything themselves: there are too many things to check each day. This means they will need to start delegating authority.

Delegating

A successful entrepreneur, used to making all the decisions about the business, can find it hard to let go of authority. But for the delegation to succeed, the subordinate must feel trusted to make decisions without interference from the boss. If the business is to grow, letting go of control can often be the single hardest challenge faced by an entrepreneur.

Maintaining effective communication

Once an organisational structure begins to develop within a growing business, communication is vital, but harder to ensure. The boss will still need to know what customers are saying or what morale is like among shop-floor staff. For this to happen, information must be able to flow upwards through supervisors and managers who may be hesitant to tell the boss about problems.

In addition, if the boss is still going to set the direction for the firm and exert a strong influence over how things get done within the business, top-down communication will be vital. But in a bigger organisation, orders and instructions may get distorted as they pass through several layers of management.

Co-ordinating far more people

In a start-up the boss is likely to know all staff on a personal level. Once the total workforce of a business passes a certain size, the boss may struggle to develop the personal relationships that had marked out their successful start-up. However, all staff (and other business resources) will still need to be heading in the same direction. It is down to the boss to ensure this still takes place, even without the ability to personally work with all members of staff on a regular basis.

Growth requires an entrepreneur to make the change from hands-on boss to leader/manager. As discussed on page 56, these two roles – manager and leader – are different. In order for effective growth to take place, the entrepreneur will have to develop management skills of co-ordination or employ effective managers who can take over this role.

Keeping an eye on the big issues

The role of leader, as explained on page 56, involves being able to understand exactly where the business should be heading and inspiring others with a vision of how the business is going to get there. As a business grows, subtle changes of direction can take place. The entrepreneur-turned-leader will need to keep an eye on the big issues facing the firm, such as what to sell and whom to sell to, while ensuring the management of resources is still taking place efficiently.

Now test yourself

TESTED

18 Why is retained profit unlikely to be a source of finance for the early stages of the growth of a business?

19 In what two ways does a loan result in cash draining out of a business?

20 Why do many entrepreneurs find delegation so hard?

Answers on p. 125

Exam practice

After a successful career in banking, Robert Southey had already started one business trading company debt and other financial products. His first business had not been as successful as he had hoped. Robert was disappointed with how little work his partner had been doing, so for his new venture he decided to 'go it alone' with Southey Capital Ltd. Much of the finance was raised with his own personal savings. Robert was keen to avoid loans as banks were not offering attractive rates of interest. With the need to build up his turnover as quickly as possible, in order to build a reputation in the markets he was dealing with, Robert's initial goal was to maximise revenue in the first year of the business. He employed four staff to help manage the office and research the deals he uncovered. However, Robert watched them like a hawk, always with a keen eye for detail and unwilling to let his business suffer from somebody else's mistake. There is no doubt that Robert has that vital skill for an entrepreneur – the ability to cope with risk – but he is not willing to take risks without trying to minimise the chances of failure. His overall strategy, of trying to minimise costs wherever possible in order to enable Southey Capital Ltd to make a profit on deals that competitors would find loss-making, is paying off.

Questions

1 Identify two benefits to Robert of starting his business as a private limited company. (2)
2 Identify two benefits to Southey Capital Ltd of having a clear business objective. (2)
3 Explain the potential opportunity costs to Robert's new business start-up of employing four staff. (6)
4 Assess whether a strategy of minimising costs is always likely to lead to business success? (10)

Answers and quick quiz 6 online

ONLINE

Summary

- Five major sources of business ideas are: observation, brainstorming, thinking ahead, personal or business experience, and innovation.
- Business opportunities may arise as a result of changes in technology, society, the economy, the housing market or the use of market research.
- The market research that precedes business start-ups will almost always be done on a very small budget.
- Common habits for successful entrepreneurs include: measuring performance accurately, stepping back from the day-to-day work, an eye for detail and loving what they do.
- The major characteristics of an entrepreneur include: understanding the market, determination, passion, resilience, the ability to cope with risk.
- The key skills required by an entrepreneur are: financial skills, persuasive abilities, problem-solving skills and networking skills.
- Major motives for starting up your own business are: profit maximisation, profit

satisficing, independence, home-working, ethical stance and social entrepreneurship.
- Objectives are targets for a business.
- A strategy must be devised to achieve objectives.
- Objectives provide a clear sense of direction for all parts of the business.
- Common objectives include: survival, profit maximisation, sales maximisation, market share, cost efficiency, employee welfare, customer satisfaction and social objectives.
- Sole traders and partnerships are legal business forms whose owners have unlimited liability.
- Limited companies can be private or public, depending upon whom shares can be sold to.
- Good decision-making requires an understanding of opportunity cost.
- Most business decisions involve trade-offs.
- As small businesses grow they face a range of problems.
- Many problems of growth are personal challenges faced as the role of entrepreneur changes to that of manager/leader.

7 Introduction to managing business activities

Finance

There is absolutely no doubt that managing money is critical to business success. The AS course explores a range of different aspects to managing money in a business:

- How to raise the money needed to start and continue running the business
- Links between different forms of business and raising finance
- Forecasting cash flows
- Forecasting sales
- Measuring sales
- Measuring costs
- Calculating profit
- Calculating the minimum level of sales needed to break even
- Forward financial planning

Three general themes of financial management are worth understanding before embarking on a detailed review of the requirements of the specification.

Working capital

REVISED

In many business start-ups, early problems arise due to a lack of **working capital**. Once an entrepreneur has raised enough finance to start up, a lot of the money will become tied up in fixed assets, i.e. property and equipment. Although fixed assets such as these are needed to run the business, other costs will need to be covered. If all the capital raised when starting the business is tied up, where will the money come from to pay wages, buy materials, pay the bills? Working capital is the money needed to cover these day-to-day costs. It is crucial that a business, large or small, ensures that it has sufficient working capital at all times.

> **Working capital** is the money that is available for the day-to-day running of the business.

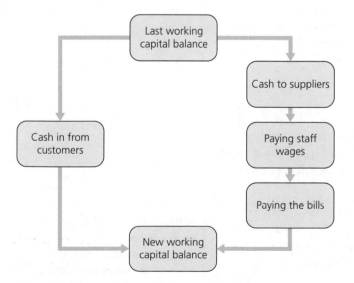

Figure 7.1 Working capital in practice

Financial management for start-ups

Financially, there are three major considerations for a new business start-up:

- How much finance is needed to open the doors on the first day's trading? Not only will the managers need to purchase or rent fixed assets, they will also need to buy enough stock, perhaps train staff and pay them while they are trained before the doors even open.
- How much will it cost to run the business? The costs will be split between the fixed costs, which need to be paid no matter how busy the business is, and the variable costs, which will change in direct proportion to the number of customers served or products sold.
- How much money can we expect to generate from selling products or services to customers? Clearly it is important to ensure that the business will be able to generate sufficient revenue from customers to cover the running costs, otherwise it is probably unwise to start the business. However, predicting just how much customers will spend is incredibly difficult for a brand new business with no track record of sales on which to base estimates.

Financial management for established businesses

For an established business, other issues will need consideration:

- Balancing cash flow and profit: Managers' success in established businesses will focus on their ability to generate profit. As will be considered in greater detail in Chapter 10, page 98, cash flow and profit are not the same thing, so situations can arise where a business appears to be successful, by generating a profit, but in fact runs out of cash; unable to pay its immediate bills, it may go bust.
- Controlling costs: Once a business grows beyond the ability of one person to make all spending decisions, some delegation of spending power is necessary. However, to prevent managers overspending, a system of budgetary control is needed. Setting up, monitoring and using budgets is a significant issue in larger firms.
- Financing growth: Once an established business is ready to grow, it faces similar issues to start-ups in generating sufficient capital to actually get the enlarged parts of the business up and running. Established firms will be able to access sources of finance unavailable to start-ups, such as retained profit, but can still fall into similar traps, such as underestimating working capital requirements.

Resources

In addition to human and financial resources, businesses need and use physical resources such as buildings, equipment and materials. These must be carefully purchased and used in order for them to generate the most profit possible.

The key to managing resources is **efficiency**. Reducing wastage in any production system is critical to running a successful business. If managers can make their organisation more efficient than their competitors, they will always have a competitive advantage in the marketplace.

Efficiency comes from generating the highest output possible from the fewest possible resources.

External issues

No business operates in a vacuum. There is a wide range of different factors outside the control of a business that have a major impact on the ability of the business to achieve its objectives. The three major areas covered within the AS course are:

- impact of the economy
- impact of legislation
- impact of the level of competition in the market.

Each has the ability to act as either a favourable or an unfavourable factor for the business.

Now test yourself

TESTED

1 Explain why entrepreneurs may often run out of working capital in the early days of their business.
2 What systems do larger firms use to control and monitor spending throughout the business?
3 What concept is key to successfully managing any business resources?

Answers on p. 125

8 Raising finance

Sources of finance: internal and external

Several circumstances may lead to a business needing to raise finance:
● Starting up
● Growing
● Dealing with a cash flow problem
● Financing extra materials needed when a large order is received

Internal sources of finance

Owner's capital: personal savings

Most likely to be used as a source of start-up finance, an owner's own personal savings, or even redundancy payment, is considered to be an internal **source of finance**. This money could be provided in the form of share capital or lent to the business as a loan.

> Places from which businesses may gain finance are referred to as **sources of finance**.

Retained profit

Once all costs have been covered and dividends paid to shareholders, any profit left is retained in the business and can be used as a source of finance. It is probably the safest and most common form of internal finance for established businesses.

> **Exam tip**
>
> As retained profit must still be available in the form of cash if it is to be used as a source of finance, look on the statement of financial position (balance sheet) for evidence that there is sufficient cash available within the business. Bear in mind that where retained profit appears on a statement of financial position, this is merely an indicator that money has been retained. It does not imply that this money is still available as a source of finance. Look instead under current assets at the cash figure.

Sale of assets

Another internal source, especially available when established businesses are changing strategy, is cash generated by the sale of assets. Especially where a firm has adjusted its strategy, there may be assets that will no longer be needed and can thus be sold in order to generate the cash necessary for other projects.

External sources of finance

Places from which a business can generate finance may also be considered as external to the business itself. These include the following:

Family and friends

In many cases, family and friends provide extra start-up capital necessary for business start-ups. This may be by taking an equity (shareholding) stake in a business set up as a limited company. Alternatively, family and friends may provide loans where banks are unwilling.

> **Typical mistake**
>
> Do not always assume that family and friends will provide interest-free loans or gifts. Those who are rich enough to consider providing finance to a friend or family member may well be so because they are financially wise enough to ensure that even in seemingly personal circumstances they do not lose out financially.

Banks

Loans to start-ups are not very common. Banks see start-ups as an extremely risky proposition. Where a loan is provided, banks will insist on some **collateral** as security, either a business asset or a personal asset belonging to an owner.

> **Collateral** is something of value that is used as security when a loan is offered. In the event of the business being unable to pay the loan back, the asset is transferred to the bank and sold in order to generate the money due for repayment.

> **Typical mistake**
>
> If the owner of a private limited company takes out a personal loan and then uses this money to invest in their business, they remain fully liable for the debt. Their decision to invest the loan made to them as an individual means that they are investing that money into the business, and the money can be lost if the business goes bust.

Peer-to-peer funding

A recent development as a source of finance, peer-to-peer funding relies on websites that can match investors willing to lend to business start-ups with start-ups needing finance. These loans will generally be at a fairly high rate of interest, but provide an option where banks are unwilling to lend.

Business angels

These are extremely rich individuals who provide capital to high-risk, small business ventures or start-ups. The Dragons in BBC's *Dragons' Den* are best thought of as **business angels**, willing to invest in risky business start-ups and become involved in the strategic management of the business in the hope of high returns.

> **Business angels** or angel investors are individuals who invest in the very early stages of a business, taking a significant equity (share) stake.

Crowdfunding

Another source of finance that has risen to prominence thanks to the internet is **crowdfunding**. It allows small investors to find business start-ups in which they are willing to invest through crowdfunding websites. No single investor is likely to be big enough to provide all the finance needed for each business using the site, but the beauty of crowdfunding is that many small investors can be gathered in order to provide all the finance necessary.

> **Crowdfunding** is obtaining external finance from many small investments, usually through a web-based appeal for investors.

Other businesses

Some businesses, especially large firms, actively seek out small businesses either starting up or in their early stages and help them out by providing finance. In return they will take a shareholding. Commonly, this practice occurs in technology-based industries with large tech firms looking to find and cash in on 'the next big thing', even if they did not develop it themselves.

Methods of finance

Loans

Loans can be provided by banks, but could also be provided by friends, family or directors of the business. A loan involves providing a lump sum of cash, which will be repaid over an agreed period of time. In addition, interest payments will also be made over the course of the loan: these represent the 'cost' of the loan. Interest rates may be variable or fixed, decided at the time the loan is taken out. Many lenders, certainly banks, will expect collateral to provide security for the loan.

Share capital

When a private company is formed, the ownership of the business is split into shares. These shares can be sold to investors who become shareholders. When the share is first sold, capital enters the business.

Venture capital

Where selling shares through the stock market or taking out a bank loan are not viable options, especially where a business opportunity is considered high risk, a **venture capital** company may provide finance, generally through a mix of loans and share capital. As the investment is high risk, the loan is likely to be at a relatively high interest rate and the venture capitalist is likely to expect a relatively large shareholding, as well as a meaningful say in decision-making. Venture capital is generally used to fund a significant period of growth for an established small business.

Overdrafts

Overdrafts offer a flexibility that other methods fail to offer. A business using an overdraft only pays interest on the overdraft when it is using the facility; in other words, when the account is negative. Admittedly the interest rate charged is likely to be higher than that on a loan but, as long as the business stays out of its overdraft most of the time, the total cost of this method of finance may not be prohibitive.

Leasing

Leasing is a sensible method of avoiding large chunks of cash outflows each time a major new asset is purchased. Although in the long term leasing will be more expensive than purchasing an asset outright, buying assets can put too great a strain on a business's cash flow.

Trade credit

Trade credit is incredibly common in business to business transactions. On average, two months' credit is offered to customers, acting as a method of financing the purchase of, most frequently, materials used in production. Not all businesses will be able to access trade credit. Start-ups or those with a poor record of payment in the past may be refused credit by suppliers.

A **method of finance** is the process through which a source of finance provides money to a business.

Typical mistake

A limited company only receives capital when each share is first sold. If the shareholder subsequently sells that share on, either privately or, for a public limited company, via the stock market, the company receives none of the proceeds of this onward sale.

Venture capital is a method of providing finance in higher-risk investments generally through a combination of loans and shares.

An **overdraft** is a facility offered by a bank to allow a customer to continue spending money even when their account becomes negative. There will be an agreed limit to the overdraft.

Leasing an asset is an alternative to buying the asset outright. Instead, the asset is rented for a monthly fee for a set period of time.

Trade credit means that goods or services provided by a supplier are not paid for immediately.

Exam practice answers and quick quizzes at **www.hoddereducation.co.uk/myrevisionnotes**

Grants

Grants are handouts, usually to small businesses, from local or central government. They are very rare, no matter what politicians claim, amounting to less than 2% of UK start-up finance. The only start-ups that may receive a grant are those likely to create jobs in areas of economic deprivation, or hi-tech firms competing with foreign rivals.

Different methods and sources of finance tend to be more or less appropriate in different circumstances. Table 8.1 summarises key issues.

Table 8.1 Methods of finance

Category	Source/method	Appropriateness
Internal sources of finance	Owner's capital/personal savings	Only relevant in a start-up or small business context
	Retained profit	The business must have made a profit and not spent it on anything else. Do not suggest this method for a new business start-up
	Sale of assets	Only for an established business – look especially for those planning to do something new, which may make existing assets redundant, thus available to sell
External sources of finance	Family and friends	Almost certainly limited to small business contexts – most commonly at start-up
	Bank	Most widely applicable source of finance, but many businesses continue to find it hard to get help from banks, certainly at reasonable interest rates
	Peer-to-peer funding	Rare, most likely to be used for a particularly risky start-up
	Business angels	Another rare source, most likely for a start-up or recently started business that may offer high rewards
	Crowdfunding	Another source that tends to be limited to start-ups rather than established businesses
	Other businesses	Rare – only a few businesses are likely to offer this and almost always in hi-tech sectors to new start-ups
Methods of finance	Loans	Note that some collateral will be needed and start-ups may find it hard to negotiate a loan at an affordable rate of interest
	Share capital	Can only be used by a limited company – sole traders and partnerships cannot sell shares without converting
	Venture capital	Only used for higher-risk businesses. They tend to be small businesses looking to achieve a significant spell of growth
	Overdraft	Only to be used infrequently – a business that uses an overdraft as a long-term source of finance will pay a lot of interest. OK for a short-term cash flow problem, not for purchasing new assets
	Leasing	Can only be used for major assets
	Trade credit	Start-ups will struggle to convince suppliers to offer them credit
	Grants	Only likely to be relevant to a business creating jobs in an area of economic deprivation or very high-tech firms trying to compete internationally

Now test yourself

TESTED

1 Identify two methods of finance on which interest must be paid to a bank.
2 Which method of finance is not available to either sole traders or partnerships?
3 Identify four common reasons why businesses need to raise finance.

Answers on p. 125

Liability and finance

The concept of limited liability was first explored on page 65. There are major implications to a business of its choice of ownership type with particular reference to the liability of owners for business debts.

Implications of limited and unlimited liability

REVISED

Table 8.2 Limited and unlimited liability

Unlimited liability	Limited liability
Sole trader	Private limited company (Ltd)
Partnership	Public limited company (PLC)

Those businesses whose owners have unlimited liability (sole traders and partnerships) are unlikely to grow significantly due to the potential downside of business problems. As the owners' liability for business debts is unlimited, they can lose all of their personal assets if the business goes into administration. This is because the businesses/people owed money can chase the owners to settle those debts incurred by their business. This can include customers who have paid in advance and not received the products or services promised, or suppliers who have supplied goods on credit but not been paid.

In many ways, this makes doing business with a sole trader or a partnership less risky because in the event of the business running into problems, customers or suppliers know that they can legally pursue the owners for debts owed.

This, though, means that running a sole trader or partnership can feel riskier as the owners have no protection of their personal assets in the event of things going badly wrong.

Owners of limited companies (shareholders) have the legal protection of limited liability. This means they cannot lose any more than they invest in the business. Without this protection, it is unlikely that businesses would grow to the size of many large businesses today. Individuals would be unwilling to take such large risks if it weren't for the protection of limited liability.

There is a downside to limited liability and that is the ability of unscrupulous individuals to set up limited liability companies, which then rack up debts before the owners place the business into voluntary **liquidation**. If it can be proved that they had fraudulent motives, then limited liability is no protection against a prosecution for fraud. However, business incompetence is not fraudulent, and if a limited company goes into liquidation and still owes money after all its assets have been sold, then those to whom money is owed may lose every penny.

> **Liquidation** occurs when a company's owners close down the company, selling off its assets to generate cash to pay off the debts of the business.

Effect of liability on sources of finance

REVISED

Sole traders and partnerships are likely to rely on the following sources of finance:
- Owners' capital
- Bank finance (loans and overdraft)
- Leasing
- Trade credit

Private and public limited companies can use:
- Share capital
- Bank finance (loans and overdraft)
- Angel or venture capital investment
- Peer to peer or crowdfunding
- Leasing
- Trade credit

For all established businesses, the most likely and probably the safest form of finance is retained profit.

Now test yourself

TESTED

4 Which two types of business offer unlimited liability to their owners?
5 What name is given to the owners of a limited company?
6 State two sources of finance that are available to limited companies but not to sole traders or partnerships.
7 Briefly explain why offering credit to a sole trader is less risky than supplying on credit to a limited company.

Answers on p. 125

Planning and cash flow

The business plan

REVISED

A **business plan** is a must for any start-up business or small business looking to grow that needs to attract external finance. Any provider of finance, whether a bank, business angel or other potential shareholder, will expect to see a carefully prepared, logical and viable plan.

Not only will the plan be useful in attracting finance, but preparation of the plan also:
- helps to ensure the entrepreneur has carefully considered potential problems
- has a reference point to maintain a clear sense of direction
- has some quantitative targets to aim for.

A **business plan** is a document setting out a business idea and how it will be financed, marketed and put into practice.

The main sections of a business plan should include:
1 Executive summary
2 The product/service
3 The market
4 Marketing plan
5 Operational plan
6 Financial plan
7 Conclusion

At the heart of the financial plan should be the cash flow forecast.

Interpreting cash flow forecasts

REVISED

The example of a cash flow forecast in Table 8.3 helps to show the key sections of the document.
- Cash inflow shows the places and timings from which cash flows into the business.
- Cash outflow shows how much cash leaves the business in each month.

Table 8.3 Example of a cash flow forecast

Month £s	March	April	May	June	July	August
Opening balance	0	3,000	(5,500)	(8,500)	(10,000)	(9,500)
Capital invested	30,000					
Cash received from sales			7,000	10,000	13,000	15,000
Cash inflow	30,000	0	7,000	10,000	13,000	15,000
Cash outflow	27,000	8,500	10,000	11,500	12,500	12,500
Monthly balance	3,000	(8,500)	(3,000)	(1,500)	500	2,500
Closing balance	**3,000**	**(5,500)**	**(8,500)**	**(10,000)**	**(9,500)**	**(7,000)**

- Monthly balance, sometimes called net cash flow, shows the net effect of the month on cash flow (cash inflow minus cash outflow).
- Opening balance (usually at the top of the table) shows the amount of cash the business had at the beginning of the month. This will be last month's closing balance.
- Closing balance shows the amount of cash in the business at the end of the month, calculated by adding the monthly balance (net cash flow) to the opening balance.

The main figures to consider when analysing a cash flow forecast are:
- Closing balance: If negative this shows the need for extra finance, quite possibly the need to arrange an overdraft so that the business can continue to spend after its bank balance has fallen to zero.
- Monthly balance (net cash flow): This will indicate how well each month is expected to go for the business.

Negative values for either of these indicate the key benefit of a cash flow forecast, such as the ability to spot problems in advance, in time to do something about them, such as arranging an overdraft or delaying a payment.

> **Exam tip**
>
> Watch out for the effects of seasonality on a cash flow forecast when you are interpreting it. Think about what type of business is being analysed before deciding whether cash flow looks dangerous. Remember that a toy firm, for which 80% of sales may be made in the run-up to Christmas, may experience poor cash flow during the rest of the year. As long as it is able to maintain a healthy closing balance, there will be enough cash to carry it through to cash-rich months.

> **Exam tip**
>
> Be careful not to over-react to one negative figure on a cash flow forecast. One bad month does not spell the end for a business. However, examiners will really be looking to see whether you can spot upward, or more likely downward, trends on a cash flow forecast. A consistent reduction in monthly balance could spell trouble.

Manipulating cash flow forecasts

REVISED

Stress-testing a cash flow forecast can be a useful analytical technique. Try calculating the effect on closing balance of one month's cash inflows being delayed. Alternatively, try judging the effect on closing balance of an unexpected cash outflow, such as an emergency repair to some equipment.

Calculating the difference between the closing balance at the end of a cash flow forecast and the opening balance at the start of the forecast gives a clear sense of the overall impact of that trading period on the cash flow. If overall balances are rising, then the business should be in a generally healthy cash position.

Exam practice answers and quick quizzes at **www.hoddereducation.co.uk/myrevisionnotes**

Noting the way the closing balances move can help to show trends. Look at Figure 8.1 to see how the future may actually be looking brighter by August, despite negative balances.

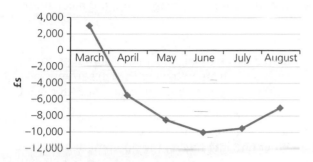

Figure 8.1 Closing balance from Table 8.3

Try to explore how much credit the business gives and receives. A poor-looking cash flow forecast can be vastly improved by chasing credit customers to pay up on time, a task that may be far easier than finding brand new customers. Alternatively a poor closing balance can be survived if the firm is able to negotiate extra credit from a supplier, to prevent cash flowing out until the next month.

Uses of cash flow forecasts

REVISED

The fundamental use of a cash flow forecast is to spot cash problems in advance so that action can be taken in time to prevent a major crisis. Examples of actions that help to improve cash flow include:

- Producing and distributing products as quickly as possible, reducing the time between paying for materials and receiving cash for finished goods
- Chasing customers to pay quickly. This could involve incentivising cash payment with a discount, or more careful credit control, such as chasing credit customers to remind them to settle their payments on time
- Keeping stocks to a minimum, as stock represents cash spent, but not yet converted back as a cash inflow
- Minimising spending on equipment, using leasing or renting as methods of finance, or even postponing investments

Limitations of cash flow forecasts

REVISED

The forecast is only as good as the estimations that have been made in order to generate the figures. Since most entrepreneurs tend to be fairly optimistic, there can be a great danger that cash inflows are forecast too high, or to arrive too predictably.

A table of figures can give the impression of factual data whereas, in reality, a cash flow forecast remains a best guess of what is likely to occur in the future. If users of the cash flow forecast trust the accuracy of the document too much, they may be lulled into a false sense of security.

Now test yourself

TESTED

8 For whom are most business plans primarily produced?
9 What forms the heart of the financial plan within a business plan?
10 What is cash inflow minus cash outflow called?
11 How can many businesses survive a short time with a negative closing cash balance?

Answers on p. 125

Exam practice

Fresh out of school, Phoebe Hart was ready to start her new business, a business she had been planning throughout her time studying Business in the Sixth Form. With no local tanning salon, but a consumer base increasingly 'beauty conscious', Phoebe's suspicions were confirmed when she found secondary research confirming strong growth in the tanning market.

Slightly worryingly, her secondary research had also revealed some major claims for damages from customers of other tanning salons who had suffered injuries and burns following their treatment. However, Phoebe was confident she could avoid these problems and set about planning how to raise the finance she needed to start up.

Her elder sister, who had been saving to buy a flat, was persuaded to lend Phoebe £10,000 at a low rate of interest, while Phoebe's other savings were also ploughed into buying the equipment and lease needed to start up. In addition, Phoebe approached her bank about arranging an overdraft to help her through quieter periods. Phoebe employed a 16-year-old college leaver to help her run the salon as he was willing to work for a low wage.

With her plans firming up, Phoebe produced a thorough business plan, which she showed to the bank. Included was a cash flow forecast. Extracts from the cash flow forecast are shown below.

	Month £s					
	April	May	June	July	August	September
Opening balance	0	(2,000)	(2,200)	(2,000)	(1,800)	d
Capital invested	15,000	0	0	0	0	0
Cash from sales	0	2,500	3,000	3,000	2,500	2,800
Cash inflow	15,000	2,500	3,000	3,000	2,500	2,800
Cash outflow	17,000	2,700	2,800	2,800	c	2,700
Monthly balance	a	(200)	200	200	(200)	100
Closing balance	(2,000)	b	(2,000)	(1,800)	(2,000)	(1,900)

Questions

1 Fill in the gaps on the cash flow, labelled a–d.   (2 marks each)
2 Explain two benefits to Phoebe of producing a business plan.   (4)
3 Assess whether Phoebe was right to start her business as a sole trader.   (10)

Answers and quick quiz 8 online

ONLINE

Summary

- Common situations in which a business needs to raise finance include starting up, growing or trying to solve a cash flow problem.
- Sources of finance can be internal or external.
- Different methods can be used to raise finance.
- Unlimited liability businesses cannot raise finance by selling shares.
- Limited companies have a wider range of sources and methods of finance available.
- Producing a detailed business plan helps attract finance.

- A business plan is also useful to the entrepreneur in planning and running their business.
- Forecasting future cash flows helps to spot problems early enough to take action.
- Several quick calculations can help to analyse what a cash flow forecast is showing about a business's finances.
- Always consider the context of the business when making judgements on what a cash flow forecast shows.

9 Financial planning

Sales forecasting

Sales forecasting forms the basis of almost all future planning. Without plans for the future, businesses would be left to simply react to changes, and fail to deliver effective products and services when consumers want them.

Purpose of sales forecasts

A range of plans will be required within a business to ensure each functional area is able to operate effectively. The sales forecast will be the basis of each of the following:

- HR plan: In order to ensure that, in the medium to long term, the right number of staff with the right skills are employed, and in the short term, the right number of staff are actually at work, the HR department will carefully consider sales forecasts.
- Marketing budgets: In order to decide how to allocate its marketing budget, a business such as Mars uses sales forecasts for each brand, to know whether to boost sales of a star such as Maltesers, or to try to revive the sales of a struggler such as the Mars bar.
- Profit forecasts and budgets: When planning how much the firm is expecting to make in revenue and profit, the basis will be accurate sales forecasts. These will help to shape expectations of spending, as shown in budgets for different departments.
- Production planning: If the business is to satisfy demand for its product or service, it will need to ensure that enough products are made, and before that, that enough raw materials are made. Planning production and inventory levels will take place by working backwards from sales forecasts.

Factors affecting sales forecasts

Consumer **trends** – tastes and habits – change as time passes. Effective sales forecasting must therefore allow for the effect on demand of these changing tastes and habits. Examples of changes in consumer tastes and habits could include:

- increased demand for more convenient foods
- a trend towards healthier eating for some consumers.

Other consumer trends may be based on:

- Demographics: The UK has an ageing population, meaning increased demand for products aimed at the elderly.
- Globalisation: This is an increased willingness to buy products, from food to holidays, which recognise the global nature of today's world.
- Affluence: Despite short-term economic problems, over the past 70 years, UK consumers have become wealthier, thus are more able and willing to spend on luxuries.
- Economic variables: As explained in detail in Chapter 3, pages 23–25, income elasticity is the calculation of the impact on demand for a product of a change in consumers' incomes. Therefore, an economic fluctuation,

> A **trend** is the general path that a variable takes over a period of time.

such as a recession, can have a major impact on sales, especially of income elastic products. Therefore, to forecast sales effectively, a business must pay attention to economic forecasts and use knowledge of its products' income elasticity to help forecast future sales.

In addition to changes in the economic cycle, changes in individual economic variables can affect sales:

● Value of the pound: A decrease in the value of the pound makes imports more expensive and may push consumers to favour UK-produced products.
● Changes in taxation: Taxes on individual items, such as petrol or alcohol, can affect demand, as well as changes in general taxation, such as the rate of VAT.
● Inflation: If inflation is higher than the rate of increase of average incomes, consumers will need to tighten their belts, spending less and damaging sales of some products and services.

Taken together, these issues mean that no sales forecast should be conducted without paying attention to expert economic forecasts. Many economic changes can have a significant effect on sales for a wide range of businesses, especially those with income elastic products and services.

> **Exam tip**
>
> Examiners love to see you combining knowledge from different areas of the specification into one argument. If answering a question about sales forecasting, you are extremely likely to be able to use income, or even price elasticity, within your argument to effectively develop the point you are trying to make.

Actions of competitors

Even harder to predict are the potential actions of competitors and the impact these may have on sales. Key competitors' actions that may affect sales are:

● Changing price: A competitor that begins to undercut our prices is likely, depending on price elasticity, to steal sales, thus rendering our sales forecast overly optimistic. If we respond by cutting prices, although we may still sell the same number of products, sales revenue may be lower than expected, affecting profit and cash flow forecasts.
● Launching new products: A competitor launching a new product, or a new competitor entering our market, can have a dramatic negative effect on forecasted sales.
● Promotional campaigns: Competitors running successful promotional campaigns to try to steal market share from our product can again leave sales forecasts looking overly optimistic.

More than any of the other factors affecting sales forecasts, the actions of competitors are usually likely to have a solely negative impact. Worryingly, they are also harder to predict than economic changes or change in consumer tastes.

Difficulties of sales forecasting   REVISED

Most sales forecasts use a technique called extrapolation, meaning assuming that past trends will continue. However, as explained above, there are many reasons why past trends can change. It is the ability to forecast these changes to past trends that marks out the best sales forecasters. In many ways, great sales forecasting is as much an art as a science, as the ability to spot future changes in trends may be impossible to find in past data.

Now test yourself

TESTED

1 State three types of plan that rely on a forecast of sales as their basis
2 List three broad categories of factors where changes may have a major influence on the accuracy of sales forecasts.
3 Explain why forecasts lose accuracy as they look further into the future.

Answers on p. 125

Sales, revenue and costs

Calculating sales volume and sales revenue

REVISED

The two ways to measure how much a business has sold are:
- sales volume
- sales revenue.

Knowing how many products have actually been sold is fairly straightforward, even for a large business, as long as the business has effective internal accounting systems. Calculating the value that those sales have generated is trickier as sales revenue is calculated by multiplying sales volume by selling price. For a business selling a range of products at different prices this adds complication. If a business sells the same product at different prices depending on where or when the product is sold, even more careful recording is needed to generate an accurate figure for sales revenue.

To boost revenue, businesses can either increase their selling price (as long as sales volume is not hit too hard) without having a major impact on sales volume, or look to increase sales volume without reducing their selling price significantly.

The choice here is likely to depend on price elasticity (Chapter 3, pages 21–23).

Exam tip

The formula for calculating sales revenue is: sales volume × selling price.

Exam tip

Notice again that using elasticity as part of an argument about a question on how to increase sales revenue can show an examiner how good you are at combining different business concepts to help build an argument.

Table 9.1 Price elasticity

Price elasticity	Change to price	Effect on sales revenue
Price elastic	Increase	Revenue falls
	Decrease	Revenue rises
Price inelastic	Increase	Revenue rises
	Decrease	Revenue falls

Calculating fixed and variable costs

REVISED

To run a successful business, managers must understand not just how much they are selling but also whether they are receiving more in revenue than it is costing to run their business. No business can survive in the long term if its costs exceed revenues. Recording and monitoring running costs is thus vital.

When calculating the costs of producing a product or providing a service, a common classification for costs is to split them into:

- fixed costs
- variable costs.

When added together, these figures allow a firm to see its total costs for a time period, which can be compared with sales revenue.

Fixed costs

These are costs that do not change as output changes. They are linked to time (e.g. rent per month) rather than to how busy the business is. Fixed costs have to be paid even when a business is not producing. However, they will be the same whether the business had a great month or an awful month in terms of sales volume.

Table 9.2 **Examples of fixed costs**

Rent	Business rates (local tax)	Management salaries
Interest charges	Advertising spending	Heating and lighting

As these costs won't change as output changes, a rise in sales will spread these fixed costs over more units, meaning the fixed cost per unit is lower. This is especially important for a business for which fixed costs are higher than variable costs.

> **Exam tip**
>
> This concept of spreading fixed costs in directly with the concept of capacity utilisation is explored in Chapter 11, page 107.

> **Typical mistake**
>
> Fixed costs *do* change as time goes by, for example the landlord may decide to put up rent next month. They are fixed in relation to the amount produced, not for ever.

Variable costs

These are costs that change in direct proportion to the level of output. So, if a manufacturer doubles the amount produced, the cost of materials will double.

Table 9.3 **Examples of variable costs**

Raw materials	Piece rate pay
Fuel costs	Packaging

> **Exam tip**
>
> Questions frequently state the variable costs of one unit of output. To calculate the total variable costs it is crucial to remember to multiply this figure by the number of units produced:
>
> **Total variable costs**
> **= variable cost per unit × number of units produced (output)**

Variable costs may not actually rise in direct proportion to output. The simplest reason is that as a business increases its output, it may be able to negotiate a lower price from material suppliers, meaning that the cost of materials may not quite double as output doubles. However, for the purposes of simple profit calculations and break-even analysis, this effect tends to be ignored.

> **Typical mistake**
>
> As variable costs are often stated 'per unit', students sometimes get confused because the variable cost per unit does not change. They are variable in the sense that the total amount spent on, say, raw materials will double if the output doubles.

Total costs

Adding together variable costs and fixed costs shows the total costs of running a business for a period of time. This is the figure that is deducted from sales revenue to calculate profit.

Analysing the proportion of total costs that is fixed against the proportion that is variable can help a business to understand the importance of boosting sales volumes. Remember that:

- A business with a high proportion of fixed costs is better off trying to boost sales volumes so that fixed costs are spread over more units of output.
- For a business with relatively low fixed costs but higher variable costs, it is easier to operate at low levels of output, since its fixed outgoings each month will be relatively low.

Now test yourself

TESTED

4 State the two ways in which the sales of a business can be measured.
5 Define fixed costs.
6 Define variable costs.
7 Explain why a business with high fixed costs should seek to maximise sales volumes.

Answers on p. 125

Break-even

Knowing the **break-even** point is useful to managers of a business as it allows them to have a minimum target of sales to aim for to ensure that they are not making a loss.

> **Break-even** describes a position where a business is selling just enough to cover its costs without making a profit.

Break-even point

REVISED

To calculate the break-even point, a business needs to know the following:
- selling price
- variable cost per unit
- fixed costs.

Break-even is calculated using the following formula:

$$\text{Break-even} = \frac{\text{fixed costs}}{(\text{selling price} - \text{variable cost per unit})}$$

The bottom line of the formula shows the amount each unit sold contributes towards covering the fixed costs of the business.

Using contribution to calculate break-even

REVISED

Selling price minus variable cost per unit (the bottom line of the break-even formula) is called contribution per unit. This figure can be used to calculate break-even:

Break-even charts

REVISED

It is possible to illustrate the break-even point on a graph, known as a break-even chart. This shows costs, revenues and therefore profit at any possible level of output for a business. On the horizontal axis, all possible levels of output are shown, while the vertical axis shows costs and revenues, measured in pounds.

The example break-even chart in Figure 9.1 shows the break-even point, which occurs at the point where total costs and total revenue are the same.

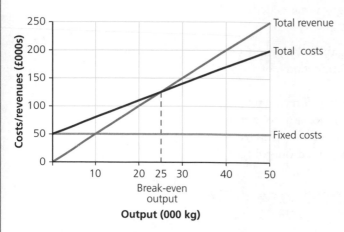

Figure 9.1 Example break-even output chart

Note the following features of the graph:
● The fixed cost line is flat, showing that fixed costs are the same at all levels of output.
● The total cost line shows the effect of adding fixed costs and variable costs together. It therefore starts on the left at the fixed cost line and moves upwards in line with the rate of increase of variable costs.
● The total revenue line begins at point (0,0) since no revenue is generated if nothing is sold.
● The break-even output is identified by dropping a vertical line down from the point at which total revenue and total costs cross to read off the amount of output that needs to be sold to cover costs.

Measuring the vertical gap between total revenue and total costs at any level of output allows the profit to be easily identified. For example, the profit when 50,000 kg is produced is £50,000.

Margin of safety

The horizontal distance between the actual output of a business and its break-even output is called the margin of safety. This shows how far demand can fall before the firm slips into a loss-making position and can be a vital figure to look out for during difficult trading periods.

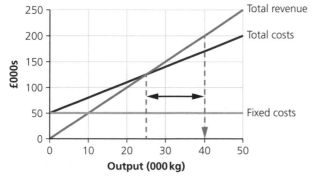

Figure 9.2 Margin of safety

Exam practice answers and quick quizzes at **www.hoddereducation.co.uk/myrevisionnotes**

Figure 9.2 shows the margin of safety if the business sells 40,000 kg. The margin of safety is 40,000 kg × 25,000 kg = 15,000 kg.

Interpreting break-even charts

In addition to showing the break-even point and margin of safety, break-even charts also serve useful planning purposes.

Being able to read off profit or loss at any given level of output can help a business plan for success or failure.

The chart can also allow other 'what if' questions to be asked, relating to what would happen to profit, break-even or margin of safety if:
● selling price is reduced or increased
● variable cost per unit reduces or increases
● fixed costs change.

Each of these requires a fresh line to be drawn on the graph, showing the effect of the possible change.

Table 9.4 Effects of change on break-even charts

What could change	What line would need to be redrawn	Direction of change	Effect on break-even point
Variable cost per unit	Total costs	Up	Up
		Down	Down
Fixed costs	Fixed costs AND Total costs	Up	Up
		Down	Down
Selling price	Total revenue	Up	Down
		Down	Up

Typical mistake

A change in sales or output does not change any lines on the graph. The effect would simply be shown by moving along the horizontal axis to read off the new figures at the new level of output.

Limitations of break-even analysis

Break-even analysis relies on certain simplifying assumptions. These may well be false in a real, dynamic business environment:
● Variable costs are assumed to increase constantly. In fact, they may increase more slowly at higher levels of output due to bulk-buying discounts.
● Break-even analysis assumes that the firm sells all its output in the same time period, which may well be untrue.
● Break-even analysis is based on a firm selling only one product at a single price.

Exam tip

Calculating the break-even point for individual products sold by a multi-product firm is quite possible, and very useful. However, this relies on splitting up the firm's **overhead costs** and allocating some to each product.

Overhead costs are those that are incurred by the business as a whole but can be difficult to attribute to a particular section of the business. For example, the costs of running Nestlé's Head Office can be hard to attribute to the actual production of any one of its hundreds of different products.

● Any break-even chart is a static model, showing only the possible situation at one moment in time. The business environment is dynamic, so break-even is not well suited to showing the effects of changing external variables such as consumer tastes or the state of the economy.

Now test yourself

TESTED

8 What formula is used to calculate the break-even point?
9 What is the formula for calculating profit using a break-even chart?
10 What three lines are drawn on a break-even chart?
11 How is margin of safety calculated?
12 If the variable cost per unit of a product decreases, what will be the effect on the break-even point?
13 What would be the effect on a firm's break-even point of deciding to cut the selling price?

Answers on p. 125

Budgets

Budgets represent the way in which most medium to large businesses manage their finances. Budgets will be set for both income and expenditure:

- Income budget: This sets a target for the value of sales to be achieved.
- Expenditure budget: This gives budget-holders a limit under which they must keep their department's costs.

A **budget** is a target for revenue or costs for a future time period.

An example of a simple budget statement is shown in Table 9.5.

Table 9.5 Example of a budget statement

	January	February	March
Income	25,000	28,000	30,000
Variable costs	10,000	12,000	13,000
Fixed costs	10,000	10,000	11,000
Total expenditure	20,000	22,000	24,000
Profit	5,000	6,000	6,000

Note that setting both income and expenditure budgets allows for a budgeted profit figure to be identified in each month.

Purpose of budgets

REVISED

- They focus expenditure on the company's main objectives for a time period.
- Expenditure budgets are set to ensure that no department or individual spends more than the company expects.
- All budgets provide a yardstick against which performance can be measured.
- Expenditure budgets allow spending power to be delegated to local managers, who may understand local conditions better and be better placed to decide how money should be spent at a local level.
- Both income and expenditure budgets can help to motivate staff in a certain department to try to hit targets.

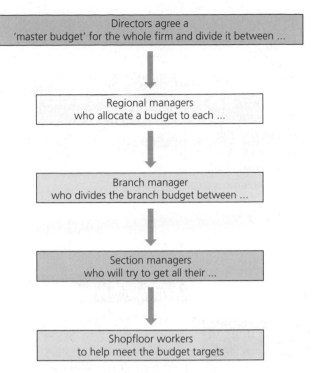

Figure 9.3 Budget holders

Types of budget

The process of setting budgets can take place in two broad ways:

- A historical budget is set using last year's budget as a guide and then making adjustments based on known changes in circumstances for the department, so if 10% more staff have been employed at a branch, that branch's income and expenditure budgets may be increased by 10%.
- Zero-based budgeting involves setting each budget to zero each year and then expects each budget-holder to justify a budget figure that they can work to for the coming year. This is very time-consuming, but can prevent the wastage that occurs if all budgets simply creep upwards year after year under a system of historical budgeting.

In reality, to prevent too much time being wasted, many businesses will use zero-based budgeting every few years before a period of historical budgeting. The result is shown in Figure 9.4.

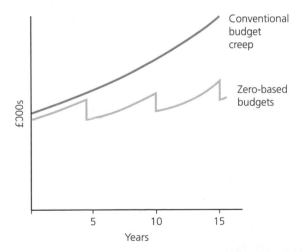

Figure 9.4 The benefits of zero budgeting: keeping costs down

Exam tip

Whichever method of setting budgets is used, perhaps a more important concept is the extent to which budgets are agreed or imposed. Imposing budgets reduces the sense of responsibility that a budget-holder feels compared to their desire to hit targets that they have agreed with their managers.

Variance analysis

Setting budgets is a helpful planning technique. However, the real power of budgets probably comes from **variance analysis**.

Variance analysis, which in most large firms will take place using a spreadsheet system such as Microsoft Excel, allows managers to spot areas where there is a significant difference between the budget and the reality. With an automated system it is possible to flag up variances of a certain size only, so that managers can focus their attention on areas with a significant variance. It is in the analysis of the causes of these variances that successful financial management tends to lie.

Variances can be:
- Adverse: The actual figure was worse than the budgeted figure.
- Favourable: The actual figure was better for the business than the budgeted figure.

Variance analysis involves looking back to calculate the difference between a budgeted figure and the actual figure that occurred.

Table 9.6 Variance analysis

Type of budget	Relationship between budget and actual	Effect on profit	Classification of variance
Income	Actual lower than budget	Lower than expected	Adverse
	Actual higher than budget	Higher than expected	Favourable
Expenditure	Actual lower than budget	Higher than expected	Favourable
	Actual higher than budget	Lower than expected	Adverse

Typical mistake

Budget variances should not be recorded as positive or negative, as an income figure higher than budget is a good thing but an expenditure figure higher than budget has a negative impact on profit. This is why the words 'adverse' and 'favourable' are used.

Budget variances can occur for three underlying reasons. Only one should really result in the budget-holder being blamed:
- The original budget was unrealistic.
- The target was not met due to factors beyond the budget-holder's control.
- The target was not met due to factors within the budget-holder's control.

Holding a manager to account for either failing to meet an unrealistic target or missing a target as a result of issues over which they had no control will only demotivate that manager and probably others within the business. Senior managers should therefore take care over investigating the causes of budget variances before taking action as a result of those variances.

Typical mistake

Whenever calculating a budget variance it is vital to note whether the variance is adverse or favourable. The answer to a question asking you to calculate a variance should be the actual size of the variance and the word 'adverse' or 'favourable'.

Difficulties of budgeting

Problems with budgeting systems can occur in several key areas:
- Setting budgets: It can be hard to ensure targets are set realistically, but also to avoid budgets creeping upwards over time.
- Agreeing or imposing budgets: Imposing budgets is far less motivating and effective than giving budget-holders a genuine say in setting their own targets, in agreement with senior managers.
- Failing to understand the causes of a budget variance: Blaming a budget-holder for failing to meet a target that turned out to be impossible is a sure-fire way of demotivating that manager.
- The costs of the system outweighing the benefits: In small businesses, there is less need for financial control to be delegated as a single boss may be able to keep an eye on all the finances without taking the time to set up a system of budgets.

Now test yourself

14 State three purposes of budgets.
15 What are the two main methods of setting budgets?
16 If actual income is lower than the budgeted figure, will the variance be adverse or favourable?
17 If actual expenditure is lower than the budgeted figure, will the budget variance be adverse or favourable?

Answers on p. 125

Exam practice

Andy Hemmings plans to set up a small firm manufacturing specialist signalling devices for use in vehicles. As an experienced entrepreneur, he has taken care to produce an accurate sales forecast. He has also carefully planned his finances, in order to identify his break-even point. In addition, he has set budgets as a way of checking the success of the business as he goes along. A range of information about his business is provided below:

Sales forecast for first three months:

    January – 1,600 units

    February – 2,400 units

    March – 3,000 units

Selling price = £20

Variable cost per unit = £8

Fixed costs = £24,000 per month

Questions

1 Using the information provided, calculate Andy's:
  (a) Break-even point   (3)
  (b) Profit or loss in January   (3)
  (c) Margin of safety in March   (3)
2 Explain two factors that may cause Andy's sales forecasts to be inaccurate.   (4)
3 Assess how useful break-even analysis will be to Andy in starting up and running his new business.   (10)

Answers and quick quiz 9 online

Summary

- Sales forecasts are at the heart of most business planning.
- Sales forecasts begin by assuming past trends will continue.
- The art of successful sales forecasting lies in being able to spot when the future will not reflect the past.
- Sales can be measured by volume or value (revenue).
- Costs of production can be split into variable costs and fixed costs.
- Total costs are calculated by adding total variable costs to fixed costs for a time period.

- The break-even point is a useful piece of information for managers.
- Break-even charts show profit or loss at any possible level of output.
- Contribution can be used to calculate profit.
- Break-even analysis has several limitations.
- Break-even analysis allows a business to ask 'what if' questions.
- Budgets are used to manage a firm's finances.
- Variance calculations allow performance to be measured against budgeted targets.
- Budget variances can be adverse or favourable.

10 Managing finance

Profit

Profit is a simple concept. What can make it less clear is when businesses report on different kinds of profit. This is done so that businesses can identify where things are doing well or badly for them, by analysing the differences between the different types of profit.

> **Profit** is the difference between the revenue of a business and the costs generated by the business during a period of time.

Calculating different types of profit

REVISED

Each type of profit is calculated after allowing for different types of cost.

Gross profit

This is a raw measure of profit that deducts the **cost of sales** from total revenue to show what is left after taking away the costs directly involved in making a product or providing a service.

> Gross profit = total revenue − cost of sales

> **Cost of sales** is the collective name given to the costs directly associated with making a product, such as materials, and costs of running the factory.

Operating profit

Fixed overheads are deducted from gross profit to calculate operating profit. This is perhaps the clearest indicator of just how well a business has been run during a year. As the name suggests, this is the profit generated by the normal operating activities of the business.

> Operating profit = gross profit − fixed overheads

> **Fixed overheads** are the costs that have to be paid no matter how well the business is performing, such as management salaries and rent on the head office.

Profit for the year (net profit)

The final measure of profit on your specification shows profit net of all costs except for corporation (profit) tax, which is usually charged at 20%.

> Profit for the year (net profit) = operating profit − (net financing cost and corporation tax)

> **Net financing cost** is the income from interest on bank deposits minus the interest charges from overdrafts and loans. It will usually be a negative number.

Ways to improve profit

REVISED

Improving profit can sound simple. There are only three basic routes:
- Increase revenue
- Reduce costs
- Do a combination of the two

Unfortunately, each choice tends to involve a trade-off. Increasing revenue can be achieved by spending more on advertising, but that pushes up costs. Reducing costs may involve making sacrifices on quality or customer service, which could damage revenue too. Put simply, this is why running a business is hard.

Statement of comprehensive income

All public limited companies are required to produce and publish a financial document known as the **statement of comprehensive income**. Most people refer to this as the profit and loss account. This is the document on which the different types of profit can be found. In addition, comparing this document with previous years allows judgements to be made about the performance of the business for the current financial year.

> A **statement of comprehensive income** is a document produced by public limited companies that shows revenue, a break-down of different types of cost and different types of profit for a year.

Measuring profitability

While profit is an absolute number of pounds, each different profit figure can only tell us so much about the performance of a business. More powerful than figures for profit are figures that show **profitability**. Profitability allows us to make meaningful comparisons between firms of different sizes in order to judge who has been more successful.

> **Profitability** states profit as a percentage of sales revenue.

Gross profit margin

This shows gross profit as a percentage of sales revenue:

$$\text{Gross profit margin} = \frac{\text{gross profit}}{\text{sales revenue}} \times 100$$

A business that is able to take relatively cheap raw materials and turn them into highly priced products would have a high gross profit margin. A good example is a coffee shop.

> **Typical mistake**
>
> Do not confuse profit (measured as a number of pounds) with profitability (measured as a percentage).

Operating profit margin

This is the main focus for the analysis of overall company performance. It shows operating profit as a percentage of sales, and therefore includes the impact that deducting fixed overheads has on profitability.

$$\text{Operating profit margin} = \frac{\text{operating profit}}{\text{sales revenue}} \times 100$$

> **Exam tip**
>
> For all profit margins, the higher the better.

Profit for the year (net profit) margin

The profit for the year (net profit) margin shows profitability after allowing for all business costs (apart from tax).

$$\text{Profit for the year (net profit) margin} = \frac{\text{profit for the year (net profit)}}{\text{sales revenue}} \times 100$$

Ways to improve profitability

In order to increase profit margins, a business faces two simple options:
- Increase selling price
- Cut costs

Increasing the selling price will increase profit margin but may decrease overall profit. This is because an increase in price may lead to a drastic fall in sales volume. The wisdom of increasing price hinges on price elasticity. For a price inelastic product, the fall in demand that results from a price rise may be so small as to be outweighed by the increased revenue per unit. However, for a price elastic product, increasing price is almost certain to reduce profits.

As explained above, cutting costs is rarely simple. Using cheaper materials or employing fewer staff can damage a company's reputation and thus revenue. Only where genuine waste can be identified and painlessly removed from the business is cost reduction likely to lead to a straightforward increase in profitability.

Distinction between cash and profit

REVISED

Profit is not the same as net cash flow. The reasons are two-fold:
- Sales revenue does not equal cash inflows.
- Costs do not equal cash outflows.

The simplest way to illustrate is to consider a business that offers credit to its customers and receives credit from a supplier. Sales revenue is recorded when a product changes hands, so selling an item on 60 days' credit generates sales revenue, but will not lead to a cash inflow for at least 60 days. Likewise, when the business buys materials on credit, the cost is incurred when the materials are delivered. However, no cash flows out until the supplier is actually paid, 30 days later.

Table 10.1 helps to illustrate this and other differences for a number of typical business transactions.

Table 10.1 Differences between cash inflows and revenue

Financial item	Cash inflow	Revenue
Cash sales made to customers	✓	✓
Credit sales made to customers	✗	✓
Capital raised from share sales	✓	✗
Charge rent on flat upstairs	✓	✓
Take out a £20,000 bank loan	✓	✗
Carry out a sale and leaseback	✓	✗

It is this difference between cash flow and profit that explains why profitable businesses can go bust when they run out of cash. Selling on credit especially can be very dangerous. As long as the bank manager believes credit customers will pay, an overdraft will still be available. However, a bank may withdraw the overdraft facility, leaving the business with no cash to pay its bills on a day-to-day basis.

Liquidity

Statement of financial position (balance sheet)

REVISED

Every year, all limited companies are required to send a statement of financial position, commonly known as a balance sheet, to Companies House. This shows what the business owns, as well as what it owes and where it got its money from.

For the AS part of your specification, the key question answered by a statement of financial position is: Does the firm have enough cash to pay its bills? This question means testing the firm's **liquidity**.

Measuring liquidity

A balance sheet shows more information than is needed to measure liquidity. If looking at a whole balance sheet, the section to be concerned with is just above halfway up – the section that shows **current assets** and **current liabilities**.

Measuring liquidity involves comparing the value of current assets against the current liabilities that will need to be paid. This can be done in two ways.

Calculating current ratio

The current ratio is a calculation that enables a simple judgement to be made about a firm's liquidity. Accountants tend to state that the ideal current ratio is 1.5:1. The formula used to calculate the ratio is:

$$\text{Current ratio} = \frac{\text{current assets}}{\text{current liabilities}}$$

This therefore means that if a company has a current ratio of 1.5:1, it will have £1.50 of current assets for each £1 of short-term debt it has. If the ratio is significantly lower than 1.5:1, this could mean that it will face problems settling its short-term debts. If the ratio is significantly higher than 1.5:1, the business could be criticised for having too much of its resources tied up in non-productive current assets.

Calculating acid test ratio

Often referred to as a tougher test of liquidity, the acid test ratio does not count inventories (or stock) as a liquid asset that can be set against current liabilities. The formula is therefore:

$$\text{Acid test ratio} = \frac{(\text{total current assets} - \text{inventories})}{\text{current liabilities}}$$

Liquidity is the ability of a business to find the cash it needs to pay its bills. The cash must be readily available either in the bank account or in the form of a payment from a customer that is due very soon.

Current assets are items the business owns that are in the form of cash or can be easily turned into cash quickly without a major loss in their value. There are three current assets: cash, money owed by customers (receivables/debtors) and stock.

Current liabilities are debts owed by the business that are due to be paid within the next 12 months. The two main current liabilities are trade creditors and overdrafts.

The ideal value for the acid test ratio is 1:1. This would mean that a firm has £1 of cash or money owed by customers for every £1 of short-term debt, so liquidity is sound. If the acid test falls far below 1:1, that really could spell trouble for a business trying to find the cash to pay its bills.

Some firms can trade on surprisingly low acid test ratios, notably Tesco, which rarely has an acid test of more than 0.5:1. This is less of a problem for a business that can generate millions of pounds through its tills every day or one that is large enough to be likely to access bank finance fairly easily when needed.

> **Exam tip**
>
> Notice that inventories form the difference between the two liquidity ratios. A company with a high current ratio but low acid test is likely to have high stock levels, which could cause a problem. The size of the problem will depend upon how quickly it can turn its stocks into cash.

Improving liquidity

Improving liquidity relies upon bringing extra cash onto the balance sheet. This could involve one or more of the following:
- Selling under-used **fixed assets** such as equipment or machinery
- Raising more share capital
- Increasing long-term borrowing through loans
- Postponing planned investments

> **Fixed assets** are items owned by the business which it intends to use over and over to generate profit. Examples include property and machinery.

Managing working capital

Figure 10.1 The working capital cycle

Figure 10.1 shows the different stages through which **working capital** passes as a business buys, produces and sells products or services. Managing this cycle, to ensure that there is always enough working capital in the system to prevent blockages or delays, is crucial to successful financial management. Actively managing the working capital cycle involves:
- ensuring there is enough money in the system altogether
- making sure cash moves through the cycle as quickly as possible.

> **Working capital** is the money that is available for the day-to-day running of the business.

If these two requirements are to be met financial managers are likely to consider the following actions:
- Control cash used. This involves keeping the amount of cash used as low as possible, by reducing stock levels, controlling credit periods

offered to customers and gaining as much credit as possible from suppliers, and getting products on sale as quickly as possible.

● Minimise spending on fixed assets. This can be helped by leasing rather than buying new assets, which prevents large outflows of cash draining working capital from the system.

● Plan ahead to estimate carefully the amount of cash that will be needed in the next few months. This will ensure that adjustments to the cycle can be made in good time.

Business failure

Ultimately, any business that fails will do so because it does not have enough cash to pay the bills. However, the reasons why businesses run out of cash can be complex. Not all, or even many, of these are caused by financial issues. It is other causes that lead to the financial problems that bring down the business. Major issues tend to focus on marketing or strategic problems such as:

● not really understanding consumers
● failing to differentiate from rivals
● failing to communicate what is special about your business to consumers
● poor leadership
● not being able to find enough ways to generate revenue.

Internal causes of business failure   REVISED

Marketing failure

Problems understanding changes in the marketplace, or even what consumers are really looking for, will lead to a shortage of revenue. Poor decisions relating to the marketing mix can often result from this.

Financial failure

Managers need to manage finances actively, planning ahead and making adjustments when necessary. Failing companies sometimes stumble into cash flow crises without seeing them coming.

Systems or operations failure

If IT systems simply do not provide the right people within the business with the information they need, things start to go wrong. If physical systems break down, such as manufacturing or ordering stock, the business will find itself unable to satisfy demand for its product and will rapidly lose customers.

External causes of business failure

Shifts in the external environment within which a business is operating can lead to business failure. In these cases, it is perhaps easier to find sympathy for business managers brought down by factors that are outside their direct control. However, really good leaders are adept at anticipating and adapting to external changes.

Change in technology

A major technological advancement can destroy a company's sales very rapidly. As its product struggles to compete against a better product, price cutting is almost assured and, ultimately, the company may fail to operate at its break-even point.

New competitor

A new rival entering a market that is able to operate far more efficiently, perhaps as a result of innovative processes or distribution channels, may cause such a large effect as to drive existing businesses out of the market and out of business.

Economic change

In times of economic downturn, orders for luxury goods tend to dry up. If economic growth does not recover quickly, some businesses will find it hard to continue operating above their break-even point – those with insufficient cash will fail.

Behaviour of banks

The banks have a vital role to play in providing finance to business:
● To fund long-term investments designed to raise competitiveness
● To provide short-term finance to help working capital management

A failure to supply credit to businesses, or forcing businesses to accept unreasonably high interest rates, can both lead to business failure. This helps to explain why banking is a crucial but controversial sector of the UK's economy.

Now test yourself

9 How can marketing mistakes lead to business failure?
10 Why are consistent stock control problems likely to lead to business failure?
11 State three external causes of business failure.

Answers on p. 126

Exam practice

Hickmet and Hickmet Ltd was a trading firm that imported speciality foodstuffs from Turkey for the UK market. In early 2017, the business failed. Analysts suggested that the failure was down to external causes. The directors were convinced there was nothing they could have done to tackle the twin external factors of:
● declining value of the pound from late 2015 onwards; and
● the arrival, in 2014, of a larger new competitor that had previously focused on importing similar products from Greece.

However, analysis of extracts from the company's accounts suggested that the directors could have seen problems coming.

Extracts from statement of comprehensive income

	2014 (£m)	2015 (£m)	2016 (£m)
Revenue	4.5	4.4	4.0
Gross profit	1.4	1.0	0.5
Operating profit	0.2	0.1	(0.7)
Profit for the year	0.1	0	(2)

Extracts from statement of financial position (balance sheet)

	2014 (£m)	2015 (£m)	2016 (£m)
Total current assets	0.8	0.6	0.5
Inventories	0.5	0.4	0.4
Current liabilities	0.3	0.4	1.0

Questions

1 For each of the three years shown, calculate:
  (a) Gross profit margin (4)
  (b) Operating profit margin (4)
  (c) Profit for the year (net) margin (4)
2 Use these results to comment on trends in the firm's profitability. (4)
3 For each of the three years shown, calculate:
  (a) Current ratio (4)
  (b) Acid test ratio (4)
4 Use these results to comment on the firm's liquidity. (4)
5 Assess the directors' view that the failure of the business was entirely due to external factors. (10)

Answers and quick quiz 10 online

ONLINE

Summary

- There are three main types of profit.
- Profit and profitability show different things.
- Cash flow and profit are not the same.
- Liquidity measures the availability of cash to meet short-term debts.
- Liquidity can be measured using the current and acid test ratios.
- Successful working capital management is the key to ensuring healthy liquidity.

- Internal causes of business failure could include poor marketing, poor financial management or systems failure.
- External causes of business failure may include technological change, the arrival of a new competitor, economic problems or the behaviour of banks.
- Ultimately most business failures are the result of the business running out of cash.

11 Resource management

Production, productivity and efficiency

The process of creating a product or delivering a service can be a crucial source of competitive advantage. Choosing how to organise production and ensuring it is efficient are vital in making sure business resources are managed effectively.

Methods of production

How to organise production tends to be a trade-off between uniformity and speed on one hand against the ability to adapt a product to meet individual customers' needs on the other.

Job production

Job production, making tailor-made products to suit customer tastes, brings benefits and drawbacks.

> **Job production** involves making one-off items to suit each customer's individual requirements.

Table 11.1 **Benefits and drawbacks of job production**

Benefits of job production	Drawbacks of job production
Can charge a higher price as products can be tailored to meet exact specifications	Cost per unit is very high, due to high level of skill and low rates of production
Work should be more interesting for staff	Finding staff with sufficient skill can be hard and pay will have to be high

Batch production

Batch production is really a kind of compromise between job production and flow production (see below).

> **Batch production** makes a group of products to one specification at a time, allowing some variation in products, yet some specialisation.

Table 11.2 **Benefits and drawbacks of batch production**

Benefits of batch production	Drawbacks of batch production
Allows variation in the product being made	More costly to set up than job production as some specialist machinery will be needed
Speedier than job production as making a batch of identical products speeds up production	Cost per unit will still be higher than flow production as machinery will need to be adjusted between batches

Flow production

Flow production allows huge volumes of output to be produced extremely quickly and cost effectively. It is likely to rely heavily on **automation**.

> **Flow production** refers to continuous production of a single, standardised product.
>
> **Automation** means using machines to complete tasks within a process.

Table 11.3 Benefits and drawbacks of flow production

Benefits of flow production	Drawbacks of flow production
Unit labour costs are extremely low	High initial costs of installing production machinery
Huge volumes allow huge demand in mass markets to be met	Products need to be identical – no tailoring to suit different tastes

Cell production

Cell production, with its roots in the Japanese philosophy of lean production, harnesses the power of group working to increase productivity, yet maintains the scope to tailor-make different variations on a product within the cell.

> **Cell production** involves organising workers into small groups or cells that can produce a range of different products more quickly than job production allows.

Table 11.4 Benefits and drawbacks of cell production

Benefits of cell production	Drawbacks of cell production
Group working allows ideas to be generated within the cell for improvements to processes	As it is still heavily reliant on people rather than automation, costs are relatively high
The small highly skilled cell can adjust products to suit customers' needs	Production volumes will not be as high as flow production

Due to the benefits and drawbacks of each, different methods are suited to different circumstances, as shown in Table 11.5.

Table 11.5 Circumstances when each production methods is at its most effective

Job	Batch	Flow	Cell
When every customer wants something unique, e.g. a wedding dress	When production has to be split into chunks, e.g. shoes in different sizes and colours	When there is consistent, high demand for a single product, e.g. the *Sun* newspaper	When there is a need for flexibility but also high production volumes, i.e. lean production
When labour costs are low, e.g. suits tailor-made in Bangkok	When labour costs are high enough to mean job production is too costly	When labour costs are high, e.g. in France or Sweden	When labour has a lot to contribute to ideas and improved efficiency
When tailor-making something adds real value, e.g. shoes for a marathon runner	When a firm wants to limit the availability of an item, e.g. Hermès with its 'Birkin' bag	When efficiency allows prices low enough to boost sales on everyday items, e.g. baked beans	When a degree of uniqueness adds value for the customer

Productivity

REVISED

Productivity generally refers to output per worker. It is the speed at which an employee completes their task. It is calculated using the formula:

$$\text{Productivity} = \frac{\text{total output}}{\text{number of workers}}$$

> **Productivity** is a measure of the efficiency of the production process. It is usually measured as output per worker per time period.

Typical mistake

Productivity is not the same as production or output. Output can be increased by simply employing more staff, working at the same rate. To increase productivity, the output produced by each worker must be improved.

Factors influencing productivity

Many factors influence productivity. The speed at which workers can produce units of output may depend on the workers or on the environment in which they are working. Key factors affecting productivity include:

- quality and age of machinery
- skills and experience of workers
- level of employee motivation.

Link between productivity and competitiveness

Higher levels of productivity lead to lower unit costs. This is because the labour cost involved in making each unit falls as workers work faster. If a worker is paid £10 per hour and makes £10 of units each hour, the labour cost of each unit is £1. If that worker's productivity doubles, the labour cost per unit would only be 50p (£10/20 units). Lower unit costs allow businesses to cut prices while maintaining the same profit margin.

Efficiency

REVISED

Efficiency differs from productivity in that it considers waste. A process may have a high rate of productivity, but generate a lot of waste. Therefore, it is not efficient. Wasted time, which is reduced as productivity rises, is certainly a factor, but a highly productive system may come with a cost in terms of quality, meaning many of the items produced are faulty and must be thrown away.

> **Efficiency** measures the extent to which the resources used in a process generate output without wastage.

Factors influencing efficiency

The factors that determine efficiency are the same as those affecting productivity. It is only the measurement that differs.

Table 11.6 Factors affecting production and efficiency

Factor affecting production	Affects productivity because	Also affects efficiency because
Quality and age of machinery	Newer machinery may work faster, and break down less	Fewer breakdowns mean fewer faults and newer machinery may produce with less variation
Skills and experience of workers	Highly skilled staff can produce things faster, while experience brings knowledge of how to complete tasks with high efficiency and quality	Skilled staff are likely to make fewer mistakes, while experience can mean staff spot the problems that lead to faults before they occur
Level of employee motivation	Motivated staff are likely to focus on the task without distraction and to work as quickly as they can	Motivation brings pride in work, so motivated staff will be careful not to make errors, and to lose concentration less

Labour intensive versus capital intensive production

The trade-off faced by firms considering how to produce their products often boils down to the extent to which they wish to rely on machines versus relying on people.

Key issues relating to **labour intensive production**:

- Labour costs will form a high proportion of total costs.
- Managing labour cost becomes critical, perhaps forcing a firm to move abroad to lower-wage countries or spend heavily on motivational methods.

> **Labour intensive production** means that a production process relies heavily on human input with little use of automation.

- Labour intensive production offers far greater scope for tailoring products to suit customers' needs, thus adding value and allowing a higher selling price.

Key issues relating to **capital intensive production**:
- Initial costs will be very high, with the need to invest in a lot of specialist machinery.
- Running costs will be relatively low.
- It may offer little flexibility in terms of product variations.

> **Capital intensive production** uses high levels of automation, reducing the role of humans as much as possible, replacing them with machines.

Now test yourself

TESTED

1 Is job production likely to be labour or capital intensive?
2 What is the key difference between productivity and efficiency?
3 State three key factors that affect productivity.
4 What formula is used to calculate productivity?

Answers on p. 126

Capacity utilisation

Having unused assets sitting around in a business producing no profit is inefficient. Therefore, businesses continually aim to operate close to full **capacity** to avoid waste and boost profitability.

> **Capacity** is the term used to describe the maximum possible output of a business.

Calculating capacity utilisation

REVISED

The formula used to calculate **capacity utilisation** is:

$$\text{Capacity utilisation} = \frac{\text{current output}}{\text{maximum possible output}} \times 100$$

A firm's capacity utilisation is expressed as a percentage figure.

> **Capacity utilisation** is the proportion of maximum capacity being used by the business.

Implications of under-utilisation of capacity

REVISED

The major negative implication of under-used capacity is that fixed costs per unit will be higher. The following worked example illustrates this:

Maximum capacity = 5,000 units per month

Total fixed costs = £10,000 per month

When capacity utilisation is 100%, fixed costs per unit = £10,000/5,000 = £2 per unit.

When capacity utilisation is only 50%, fixed costs per unit = £10,000/2,500 = £4 per unit.

That means that with under-used capacity, a greater amount of the revenue generated by each product must be used to cover fixed costs. This reduces operating margins significantly.

In addition, under-utilisation of capacity can:
- lead to fears for job security among staff, damaging motivation
- cause poor morale among managers
- contribute to a poor reputation for the business, especially in the service sector; imagine a restaurant that usually has many tables empty even during busy periods.

> **Typical mistake**
>
> Given the implications of capacity utilisation for fixed cost per unit, some students falsely believe that all businesses should try to reach 100% capacity utilisation at all times. There are problems associated with this, as shown by the implications of over-utilisation of capacity (below).

Implications of over-utilisation of capacity

REVISED

If capacity utilisation stays close to 100% over a long period, two potential problems arise:

- The firm may be unable to accept any new orders, potentially turning away new customers to rivals.
- There will be little or no time to carry out maintenance on machines or train staff.

The ideal level of capacity utilisation is therefore close to 100%, without ever staying at 100% for a long period.

Ways of improving capacity utilisation

REVISED

There are two basic ways to boost the proportion of maximum output being used:

- Increase current output: This is likely to be accomplished using marketing methods to boost the volume of sales made by the business, perhaps through advertising or cutting the selling price. Alternatively, the business could use its capacity to make products for other businesses looking to subcontract work.
- Reduce maximum capacity: This will involve selling off assets or laying off staff. Although redundancies can be costly in the short term, reducing maximum capacity reduces fixed costs.

Now test yourself

TESTED

5 What formula is used to calculate capacity utilisation?
6 How does a high capacity utilisation help to boost profitability?
7 State two reasons why 100% capacity utilisation can be a problem.
8 What are the two basic solutions to under-utilisation of capacity?
9 If a business has monthly fixed costs of £120,000, a maximum monthly output of 1,000 units, and a contribution per unit of £250, calculate profit when:
  (a) The firm is operating at 100% capacity utilisation
  (b) The firm is operating at 60% capacity utilisation
  Assume all output is sold.

Answers on p. 126

> **Exam tip**
>
> If the causes of under-used capacity are short term, for example poor weather, it would be foolish to reduce maximum capacity. Instead, the solution is likely to lie in boosting current demand using marketing methods. If, however, the causes are long term, such as a change in consumer lifestyles, a longer-term solution – such as reducing maximum capacity – would be more appropriate.

> **Stock** or **inventory** is the name given to the materials, partially made products and finished goods owned by a business, which have not been sold.

Stock control

Stock or inventory is often viewed as a necessary evil in business. Holding stock costs money and ties up cash, but with no stock, production can grind to a halt or customers may be disappointed.

Interpreting stock control diagrams

REVISED

One method used to help control stock levels is a stock control diagram. A typical stock control chart is shown in Figure 11.1.

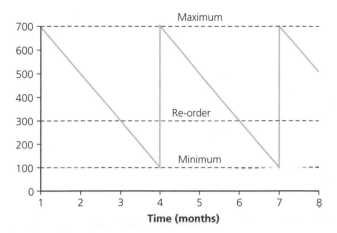

Figure 11.1 Stock control diagram

Key features of the diagram include:
- The maximum stock level set by the business, strongly affected by the amount of space available and the firm's stock-holding policy.
- The minimum or buffer stock level, i.e. the amount of stock of that item that the business aims to always have available.
- The re-order level, which is the amount at which a new order for stock is triggered.
- The re-order quantity, which is the vertical jump upwards in stock level that occurs at the start of months 4 and 7 on the diagram. This is the amount of stock that is ordered each time an order is placed.
- The lead time, or delivery time, which is the horizontal gap between a re-order being placed and the delivery of stock arriving – in this case, one month as stock is re-ordered at the start of months 3 and 6 and arrives at the start of months 4 and 7.

> **Exam tip**
>
> On a stock control diagram, any vertical gaps or changes refer to the quantity of stock. Any horizontal distances are times.

Buffer stocks

REVISED

Most businesses aim to keep minimum stock levels of raw materials used in production and also, in many cases, finished goods at all times. The reasons for this are shown in Table 11.7.

Table 11.7 Reasons for keeping buffer stocks

Reasons for keeping buffer stock of raw materials	Reasons for keeping buffer stock of finished goods
If deliveries are delayed, buffer stock allows production to continue	Helps to ensure that the business can always supply customers when they need a product, with the right size or colour
If a batch of supplies is found to be faulty, the buffer stock can be used to continue production	Allows the firm to accept rush orders from customers

Implications of poor stock control

REVISED

Effective stock control is focused on always maintaining the 'right' level of stock. The 'right' level, however, varies from business to business. Get it wrong and the business can end up with too much or too little stock. Each causes a number of problems.

Too much stock leads to the following problems:
- Opportunity cost: This ties up capital, as stock prevents that money from being used in other ways.
- Cash flow problems: Stock represents cash that has been converted into stock but not yet converted back into cash. Hold too much stock and there is a danger the firm will run short of actual cash.
- Increased storage costs: Keeping stock costs money; it needs space, perhaps security, or even refrigeration costs.
- Increased financing costs: If stock has been purchased using any form of borrowing, the business will experience extra interest costs.
- Increased wastage: Too much stock may lead to stock 'going off', or becoming obsolete.

Too little stock could cause the following problems:
- Lost customers: If an order or customer arrives expecting to receive their products immediately and there is none in stock, that customer or order may be lost to competitors.
- Delays in production: If there are no materials to process, machinery and workers may be left standing idle until the next delivery arrives.
- Loss of reputation: This may occur if word gets around that the business struggles to maintain enough stock to meet customer needs promptly.

Just-in-time stock management

Just-in-time stock management, with no buffer stock, relies entirely on frequent, small deliveries of materials from suppliers being delivered without delay and without any quality problems. This brings many benefits, eliminating costs involved in stock-holding, but increases the danger of production halting due to a lack of materials.

Key issues to consider for a firm using just-in-time stock management:
- Suppliers must be willing to deliver frequently (often several times a day).
- Deliveries must be absolutely reliable; missed deliveries leave the firm without stock.
- Suppliers may need to relocate close to the company using just-in-time.
- Will smaller, more frequent deliveries lead to a loss of bulk-buying discounts?
- Will frequent deliveries lead to increased congestion and pollution from lorries?

> **Just-in-time stock management** is a Japanese-rooted approach to stock management that aims to eliminate buffer stock completely.

> **Exam tip**
>
> Overall, the introduction of just-in-time stock management increases the importance of the relationship between a business and its suppliers. Look for evidence in any case study of how well a company gets on with its suppliers to help decide whether a switch to just-in-time would work well.

Waste minimisation

Waste minimisation is a just-in-time approach that helps to reduce waste in several ways:
- Less stock is held, meaning there is far less likelihood of stock wastage.
- Cash is not tied up in stock, effectively wasting it.
- Removing buffer stocks helps to highlight bottlenecks and problems in production processes. These can be ironed out by adjusting the production system.

> **Waste minimisation** is the aspect of lean production that to focuses on reducing waste in any business process, such as wasted time, labour on materials.

Competitive advantage from lean production

Lean production, featuring just-in-time stock management, continuous improvement linked with total quality management, as well as cell production, can improve how businesses are run in a number of ways:

- More input from staff
- A focus on quality
- Fewer wasted resources through just-in-time and total quality management
- A focus on reducing wasted time, so speed can become a source of competitive advantage

These features lead to the following sources of competitive advantage:

- Higher levels of productivity, reducing labour cost per unit
- Less space used to hold lower stock levels, reducing fixed costs
- Higher quality, leading to reputational advantages and greater repeat custom
- Faster development of new products, allowing the firm to be first to market with new ideas

> **Lean production** is a collective term for a range of Japanese techniques designed to eliminate waste from business processes.

Now test yourself

10 What name is given to the minimum level of stock a business aims to keep at all times?
11 How does a stock control diagram show the time taken to deliver by suppliers?
12 State three problems of having too much stock.
13 State two problems of having too little stock.
14 Briefly explain how introducing just-in-time stock management increases a firm's reliance on suppliers.
15 How would an increase in the level of production for a short time show up on a stock control diagram?

Answers on p. 126

Quality management

When consumers buy a product or service, they expect it to be of a certain quality. At a minimum level, customers expect the product to be fit to perform the purpose for which it was bought. Some businesses use quality as a point of differentiation.

There are three main methods of managing quality.

Managing quality

Quality control (QC)

This system involves checking output to find any faults in a production system. It is the traditional method used and relies on inspecting output, with inspection carried out by a person not involved in working on or making the products.

Quality assurance (QA)

This system focuses on producing methods to prevent quality problems arising. These methods are checklists or procedures that form a part of company policy. If employees follow these procedures, the systems are designed to prevent any quality problems.

> **Typical mistake**
>
> Too many students suggest that quality assurance ensures top-quality products. In reality, quality may simply be okay; what will be excellent are the systems of paperwork designed to try to manage quality.

Total quality management (TQM)

This is less of a system and more a way of encouraging all staff to think about the business. In order for this to work, everyone in the organisation has to understand and 'buy into' the idea of getting things 'right first time'. Quality becomes a part of everybody's job, not just production workers, but designers, accountants and sales people.

Table 11.8 Pros and cons of TQM, QC and QA

	TQM	Quality control (QC)	Quality assurance (QA)
Pros	• Should become deeply rooted into the company culture, e.g. product safety at a producer of baby car seats • Once all staff think about quality, it should show through from design to manufacture and after-sales service, e.g. at Lexus or BMW	• Can be used to guarantee that no defective item will leave the factory • Requires little staff training; therefore suits a business with unskilled or temporary staff (as ordinary workers don't need to worry about quality)	• Makes sure the company has a quality system for every stage in the production process • Some customers like the reassurance provided by keeping records about quality checks at every stage in production; they believe they will get a higher-quality service and may be willing to pay more
Cons	• Especially at first, staff sceptical of management initiatives may treat TQM as 'hot air'; it lacks the clear concrete programme of QC or QA • To get TQM into the culture of a business may be expensive, as it requires extensive training among all staff, e.g. all British Airways staff flying economy from Heathrow to New York	• Leaving quality for the inspectors to sort out may mean poor quality is built in to the product, e.g. clothes with seams that soon unpick • QC can be trusted when 100% of output is tested, but not when it is based on sampling; Ford used to test just one in seven of its new cars – that led to quality problems	• QA does not promise a high-quality product, only a high-quality, reliable process; this process may churn out 'okay' products reliably • QA may encourage complacency; it suggests quality has been sorted, whereas rising customer requirements mean quality should keep moving ahead

Quality circles

The people involved in doing a job tend to have real expertise in getting that job done. This expertise includes understanding how they could get the job done even better. Giving staff a formal system for discussing these improvements in their working area – a **quality circle** – encourages an approach of continuous improvement throughout the business.

> A **quality circle** is a group of staff who meet regularly to find quality improvements.

Exam tip

Involving staff in quality circles can be highly motivating. Look to tie in answers about this effect with the work of either Maslow or Herzberg.

Continuous improvement (kaizen)

REVISED

Whereas automation is an attempt to get a big leap forward in productivity, continuous improvement encourages staff to put forward a stream of small ideas on how to do things better. Empowering staff to make changes to their working systems brings quality and productivity improvements.

Based on cell production, each small group of employees becomes expert in their area and best placed to find improvements.

Key aspects of continuous improvement are:
- cell production
- quality circles
- small but frequent changes
- regular suggestions
- quality and productivity improvements.

Competitive advantage from quality management

REVISED

Spending money on quality management systems to ensure high quality production and service delivery brings rewards:
- It allows a price premium to be charged (often greater than the extra cost of producing high quality).
- It helps to gain distribution, with retailers confident they will not need to deal with product returns and refunds.
- It creates brand loyalty and repeat purchase.
- It can help to build a brand reputation that spreads to other products within a firm's portfolio.

Now test yourself

TESTED

16 Who is responsible for ensuring quality in a quality control system?
17 What type of production is ideally suited to a system of continuous improvement?
18 What name is given to the meetings where small groups of staff discuss possible improvements within their area?
19 What is the main source of ideas for improvement in a kaizen system?
20 How can each of the four benefit, of quality management listed above lead to increased profits?

Answers on pp. 126–7

Exam practice

Evaluate the likely impact on a UK-based manufacturer of high-quality, branded clothing of introducing a system of lean production.

(20)

Answers and quick quiz 11 online

ONLINE

Summary

- Job, batch, flow and cell production all have pros and cons, meaning each is best suited to different circumstances.
- Increasing productivity leads to lower costs per unit.
- Efficiency differs from productivity in that it measures wastage as well as speed.
- Firms face a choice between labour or capital intensive production methods.
- Capacity utilisation has major impact on fixed cost per unit and thus profit margins.
- Increasing capacity utilisation can be done through increasing current output and sales or reducing maximum capacity.

- Stock control diagrams can be used to help manage stock and show a range of different features of stock management.
- Firms can face problems from having either too much or too little stock.
- Just-in-time stock management aims to eliminate buffer stock.
- Lean production is an approach to production that includes JIT, TQM, cell production and continuous improvement.
- Quality management systems include quality control, quality assurance and total quality management.
- Good quality management can bring competitive advantage.

12 External influences

Economic influences

Effects on the business of economic changes

The economic environment within which businesses operate can have a major impact on both revenues and costs. It is therefore a vital determinant of profit. Changes in several key economic variables influence business performance in different ways.

Inflation

If prices are rising throughout an economy, the costs paid by a business for raw materials, property and labour (wages) will be rising. However, if consumers are used to prices rising, firms may be able to increase their selling prices in order to protect profit margins. The circumstances in which **inflation** has a major effect are:

- when rates of inflation are significantly above 2%
- when prices are rising faster than average earnings
- when UK inflation is higher than that in most other countries.

> **Typical mistake**
>
> If the rate of inflation is falling, say from 2% to 1%, prices are not going down. They are simply rising more slowly. Deflation – a situation where average prices are falling – is rare in the UK and would be shown by a negative rate of inflation, e.g. –1.5%.

> **Inflation** is the percentage rate at which average prices rise during a year within the whole UK economy.

> **Typical mistake**
>
> Too many student answers to questions on inflation simply consider the effect of inflation on costs, ignoring the fact that firms may well be able to increase their selling prices to protect profit margins.

Effects of inflation on businesses

- A firm with a long-term fixed price contract may find that if costs rise rapidly while the contract is being completed, the fixed price does not even cover its higher level of costs, damaging profitability.
- Firms with substantial long-term borrowings will find the real value of the money they repay will be lower following a period of high inflation, as inflation has the effect of reducing the real value of money.
- If inflation in the UK is higher than in other countries, UK businesses may lose competitiveness against foreign rivals whose costs are likely to be rising more slowly. This would allow foreign firms to charge lower prices.

> **Exam tip**
>
> Look for evidence of a company's revenues and costs being affected differently by inflation to show whether profits would be harmed or not. If many resources are imported from countries with low inflation, costs may be rising more slowly than the business can push up domestic selling prices, meaning profit margins may actually rise due to inflation.

Exchange rates

It is changes in the **exchange rate** of the pound that will affect UK businesses. Most directly affected will be UK businesses that export their products and services, and UK businesses that buy materials or other supplies from abroad.

> An **exchange rate** is the value of one currency expressed in terms of another.

Effects of exchange rates on businesses

Table 12.1 Summary of effects of exchange rate changes

	Example	Impact on exports	Impact on imports
£ appreciates	£1 was $1.60 but now buys $1.80	UK exports get pricier, so sales volumes slip	Imports to UK get cheaper, making it harder for UK firms to compete
£ depreciates	£1 was at €1.30 but now slips to €1.15	UK exports get cheaper, so sales volumes rise	Imports to UK get more expensive, so UK firms can compete more effectively

A handy way to remember the effect of a stronger pound is the word SPICED:

- **S**trong
- **P**ound
- **I**mports
- **C**heaper
- **E**xports
- **D**earer

Interest rates

Although different lenders will charge different **rates of interest**, most will adjust their rates in line with those charged by the Bank of England. This is why the Bank of England's base rate is such an important economic variable.

> A **rate of interest** is the amount charged by a lender per year for borrowing money. This is expressed as a percentage of the amount of money outstanding.

Effects of interest rates on businesses

An increase in interest rates tends to have negative effects on businesses in four ways:

- Consumers are likely to have less money to spend as payments on mortgages or other borrowings will increase. This is likely to reduce demand.
- The amount paid in interest on any borrowing by the business will rise, pushing up costs.
- Consumers are less likely to 'borrow to buy', so products that are often bought on credit, such as cars or sofas, will see demand fall, as the credit will cost more.
- Businesses are less likely to invest as the opportunity cost of investment (keeping the money in the bank to earn interest with no risk) will be greater.

Reducing interest rates is likely to have the same effects in reverse, being mainly beneficial to businesses.

Taxation and government spending

In the UK, government spending (on the NHS, defence, education, etc.) accounts for roughly 40% of all spending in the economy. So government decisions on spending and how to raise the money to spend (taxation) have a major impact on businesses.

Many private sector businesses are largely dependent upon the state for their income, such as:

- publishers of textbooks
- road-building firms

- pharmaceutical firms (producers of medicines)
- railway companies (given government subsidies).

Companies in general tend to press governments to cut their spending (and taxes), but many are heavily dependent on that government money.

Effects of taxation and government spending on businesses

Governments change levels of taxation and government spending to try to manage the economy. Their goal is to create stable economic growth. Table 12.2 shows government aims combined with the effects of changes in taxation and government spending.

Table 12.2 The impact of a change in taxation and government spending

	Government spending up	Government spending down	Government puts taxes up	Government puts taxes down
To help reduce the level of unemployment	Extra spending on road-building, health and other services with big workforces			Reduce income tax to enable families to keep and spend more of the money they earn
To cut the growth rate when it is rising too fast		Cut the spending on health, education and defence, to take a bit of spending from the economy	Increase income tax to force people to think harder and more carefully about what they buy	
To improve the competitiveness of British firms	Extra spending on education			Cut company taxation (corporation tax)
To cut the rate of imports, especially of consumer goods		Cut benefits, e.g. state pension, to reduce people's ability to buy exports	Increase VAT on all goods other than food and drink	

The business cycle

Economic growth does not tend to follow a stable path. At times, economies grow quickly; at other times, growth is slower, or economies even shrink from year to year. The pattern of economic growth in the UK tends to follow a pattern where strong growth (boom) is followed by periods of recession, where the economy actually contracts.

Effects of the business cycle on businesses

The key impact that the business cycle has on businesses is primarily related to demand for products. If the economy slows, consumers will, on average, reduce their spending, while in a boom period, consumer demand rises rapidly. Changes in consumers' incomes are the result of changes in wages or even changes in the level of unemployment.

The effect of the business cycle on businesses is therefore mainly dependent on one thing:
- income elasticity of demand.

This was covered in depth in Chapter 3, pages 23–25. Table 3.5 summarises the effect of the changes in income brought on by economic boom and economic recession, according to the income elasticity of the product being sold.

Effect of economic uncertainty

Predicting the economy is a little like trying to predict sales for every business in the UK. In Chapter 9, pages 85–87, we explored why forecasting sales of just one product is difficult. It is therefore vital to remember that forecasting the economy is an inexact science.

Business decision-makers love certainty. When devising plans for investment over the next five to ten years, directors want to be sure that the money they spend will be recovered and generate a profit. Uncertainty means they cannot be sure. In Chapter 2, page 11, we explored the reasons for uncertainty. Featuring high on the list of reasons for uncertainty in business, along with the reasons why sales forecasting is difficult, is economic change.

No business decision-makers will make any long-term decisions without thinking first about the likely state of the economy in the future. Therefore, business leaders prefer economic stability to the uncertainty that comes with cyclical economic growth.

Now test yourself

1 Briefly explain what is happening to prices when the rate of inflation falls from 2% to 1%.
2 Why can many businesses maintain profit margins during times of inflation when their costs are rising?
3 Which word is helpful in remembering the effects on UK businesses of a stronger pound?
4 Identify three ways in which an increase in interest rates has a negative effect on businesses.
5 What type of products find sales particularly hard hit during a recession?

Answers on p. 127

Legislation

Laws passed by parliament are needed to ensure that businesses behave in what is generally considered to be an acceptable way. Although many specialist areas of the law exist covering business activities, the five main areas in which legislation affects business are explained below.

Effects of consumer protection laws on business

The main goal of consumer protection legislation is to ensure that businesses actually deliver on what they promise the consumer.

Aspects of this include:
- Does the product do what it claims to do?
- Is the product correctly labelled?
- Is the product sold in the correct weight or measure?
- The rights of consumers to refunds or to exchange faulty products.

The driving force behind consumer protection legislation is to ensure that no business can gain an unfair advantage over its rivals through deceitfulness. Ultimately, competition should be based on the product and price at which it is sold, not claims that bend the truth.

Two major Acts of Parliament covering consumer protection are:
- the Sale of Goods Act
- the Trade Descriptions Act.

Exam tip

Many argue that businesses that mistreat customers will ultimately gain a poor reputation and lose business, making consumer protection legislation unnecessary. However, too many examples exist of 'cowboys' who mistreat customers, then set up under another name to rip people off again, to suggest that these laws are unnecessary.

Effects of employee protection on business

Employee protection law aims to state and uphold minimum standards of treatment that employees can expect from their employer. Major issues covered include:

- fair pay
- sick leave
- maternity and paternity leave
- employment contracts
- relationships with trade unions
- the ability of businesses to get rid of staff
- the responsibilities of businesses to employees who are made redundant.

Almost all businesses would prefer less protection for staff, since this gives them greater flexibility in terms of their human resources. Businesses tend to argue against increased rights for workers, claiming that increased costs will result and this will make it harder for them to compete with international rivals. A summary of the effects on businesses of employee protection legislation is shown in Table 12.3.

Table 12.3 Implications of employment legislation

Key area of employment law	Possible implications for firms
Minimum wage	Increased labour costs, which may lead to increased automation in the longer term and increased unemployment; on the plus side, employees may be more motivated by a fair wage satisfying basic needs
Right to a contract of employment	Meets employees' security needs but can reduce employers' flexibility in how they use their staff
Increased right to sick, maternity and paternity leave	Increased cost of paying for cover for these staff; however, staff may feel more valued as they feel well treated by employers, reducing staff turnover levels, which saves the costs of recruiting new staff
Redundancy	Reducing capacity becomes expensive due to statutory payments to staff made redundant; this can mean that closing a factory or office has a negative impact on cash flow in the short term
Trade union rights	Employers can be forced to deal with a trade union if enough staff are members; this does bring benefits as well as drawbacks

Effects of environmental protection on business

Given the broadly accepted need to regulate the effect of business on the environment, a range of legislation now governs how businesses treat the natural environment. Major areas include:

- materials that firms must use for certain products
- processes firms are allowed to use to make certain products
- the need to use recyclable materials for certain products
- landfill tax
- the need to carry out environmental risk assessments for different parts of a business's activities.

Once again, businesses tend to resist new, tougher legislation, claiming it will increase their costs in a way that foreign rivals will not have to cope with.

Much of the recent legislation on the environment came from the European Union. Now that Britain has voted to leave the EU, the UK

Exam practice answers and quick quizzes at **www.hoddereducation.co.uk/myrevisionnotes**

government will have to replace many of the EU laws that governed the way UK businesses had to treat the environment. Businesses and many others will be interested to see what decisions are taken.

Effects of competition policy on business

When businesses compete with one another, they tend to keep prices at a sensibly low level, provide a good service and generate new innovative products and services. With no competition, prices can be pushed high, service standards can slip and innovation can dry up. Therefore, governments seek, through legislation, to ensure that there is competition in all markets. The key legislation is the creation in 2014 of a government-funded body called the Competition and Markets Authority (CMA). The CMA is responsible for:

- investigating proposed takeovers and mergers
- investigating allegations of anti-competitive practices
- taking legal action against those who collude to maintain high prices within a market, such as **cartels**.

A **cartel** is a group of companies operating in the same market who make agreements to control supply and thus prices.

Figure 12.1 Functions of the CMA

The work of the CMA should, indirectly or directly, ensure that:

- companies have to set competitive prices
- companies do not collude with others in their market to the detriment of consumers
- mergers and takeovers that will create overly powerful firms are prevented.

Effects of health and safety on business

Health and safety law is designed to protect employees and customers in the workplace. The major piece of legislation – the Health and Safety at Work Act 1974 – places the burden on employers. Key aspects of this burden are:

- safe physical conditions
- precautions that firms are required to take when planning their work
- the way in which hazardous substances should be treated in the workplace.

Complying with health and safety legislation has both positive and negative effects on businesses as shown in Table 12.4.

Table 12.4 Positive and negative effects of health and safety legislation on businesses

Positive effects on businesses	Negative effects on businesses
Should prevent incidents that create negative publicity	Extra paperwork
Should help to motivate employees, who feel safe	Need to pay for extra safety equipment
Accidents can delay or halt production – these should be avoided	Need to pay to adjust physical work conditions

The role of the publicly funded body, the Health and Safety Executive, is to find and prosecute companies guilty of major breaches of this legislation.

> **Exam tip**
>
> In spite of the fact that legislation exists to prevent unscrupulous firms stealing an advantage, illegal practice still occurs. Although some may argue that consumers will avoid these firms, forcing them out of business, virtually no businesses are forced to close as a result of breaking the laws that govern business. It can be argued that the penalties for breaking the law are simply not strong enough.

Now test yourself

TESTED

6 State two potential impacts on a business of complying with new, tougher environmental legislation.
7 What is the name of the organisation responsible for enforcing health and safety legislation?
8 Whose responsibility is it to ensure employees work in a safe environment?
9 State two areas the Competition and Markets Authority can investigate.

Answers on p. 127

The competitive environment

The number of businesses supplying products or services in a market can have a major effect on how businesses operate. From monopoly markets with only one dominant supplier to fiercely competitive markets with many businesses fighting one another for consumers, business behaviour can vary dramatically.

> The **competitive environment** experienced by a business refers not just to how many competitors it faces, but to how directly other firms' products are in competition and how fierce rivalries are.

> **Exam tip**
>
> The best exam answers recognise the level of competition within the market, suggesting courses of action appropriate to the level of competition found in the market being examined.

Competition

REVISED

One dominant business

A market dominated by a single business, described as a **monopoly**, is bad for consumers because:
- Consumers have little choice.
- Prices tend to be high.
- There is little incentive for the dominant firm to innovate or provide great customer service.

As described on page 119, governments generally try to prevent monopolies occurring to prevent consumers suffering.

> A **monopoly** is a single business that dominates supply in a given market.

However, companies strive to become an effective monopoly. A key focus of this activity is trying to build barriers to entry that prevent new firms entering the market. Examples of possible barriers to entry include:
- patents and technological breakthroughs
- incredibly strong brands and high advertising budgets
- heavy spending on infrastructure (such as mobile phone network masts).

Competition between a few giants

In an **oligopoly** market, rivalries are intense, as it is clear that in most cases one firm can only gain market share by directly taking it from one of just a handful of rivals.

Given the intense rivalries, it may appear odd that companies in an oligopoly rarely compete on price. The reason is that they fear a price war would start, leading to lower profit margins for all in the industry. Instead, non-price competition exists, focusing on aspects such as:

- branding
- product features
- product design
- advertising
- technical innovations.

> An **oligopoly** is the name given to a market dominated by just a few major suppliers.

The fiercely competitive market

These markets tend to be characterised by many small businesses competing with one another, often on the basis of price. This keeps profit margins low and ensures consumers usually get a bargain. However, a business that is able to find an effective method of differentiation within a fiercely competitive market will stand a far better chance of success.

Many of these markets tend to be for commodity products which, by definition, are hard to differentiate. For businesses selling these, there may be little choice of strategy other than keeping costs as low as possible in the hope of undercutting rivals' prices and still making some profit.

Market size

REVISED

Big markets

Larger markets, even those with a few fairly dominant firms, offer scope for new competition, usually through carving out a niche. Therefore in a large market there is likely to be a fair degree of competition. This is likely to keep even dominant producers from becoming complacent, as they recognise the need to offer good service to avoid opening an opportunity to a rival.

Small markets

In a smaller market, with fewer customers and lower total sales, it may be easier to build up barriers to entry, carving up the market between just a few businesses.

Markets whose size is changing

Markets tend to grow or shrink in size over time. Predictably, the direction of this change in size will affect the level of competition:

- Growing markets … attract new entrants … seeking higher profits on offer.
- Shrinking markets … see established firms exiting … as profitability tends to be low and thus unattractive.

Business responses to a tougher competitive environment

REVISED

When new competitors arrive, or the intensity with which an existing rival is fighting increases, businesses face a choice of how to respond.

Price cutting

Attracting new customers, or hanging on to existing customers, could be achieved by cutting the selling price. Unless this is accompanied by cutting the costs of production, profit margins will fall. This is why price cutting is rarely a successful long-term answer.

Increased product differentiation

Finding or stressing new ways to show that our product is different to those of our existing or new rivals is likely to be the key to success in a tougher environment. Methods of product differentiation could include:
● branding
● product features
● product design
● advertising
● technical innovations.

Collusion

Through desperation or deliberate cunning, companies trying to survive in a really tough competitive environment may be tempted to behave illegally. It is easy to understand why a desperate business may be willing to break the law in this way. It is harder to see it as a sensible choice, given the strength of anti-**collusion** legislation in the UK.

> **Collusion** occurs when two or more rival businesses agree to fix supply or prices within their market. This is illegal.

Now test yourself

TESTED

10 What name is given to a market dominated by just a few large companies?
11 State two reasons why monopolies tend to be bad for consumers.
12 List three methods of non-price competition.
13 What is meant by a barrier to entry?

Answers on p. 127

Exam practice

Evaluate whether uncertainties in the current external environment in the UK mean that business success is, more than ever, down to luck rather than good decision-making. (20)

Answers and quick quiz 12 online

ONLINE

Summary

● The major economic changes that can affect businesses are: the business cycle; government spending and taxation; inflation; exchange rates; interest rates.
● Economic change is a source of great uncertainty for business decision-makers.
● There are five main areas in which the law can affect businesses: consumer protection; employee protection; environmental protection; competition law; health and safety.

● Most changes to the law lead to an increase in costs for a business.
● The competitive environment faced by a business will affect its strategy.
● The number of firms in a market affects the degree of competition.
● The size and growth rate of a market affect the degree of competition.
● Firms can compete on price and non-price aspects, including branding, advertising, product features, design and innovation.

Now test yourself answers

Chapter 1

1 (a) Apple's iPhone: design
  (b) Heinz Tomato Ketchup: quality of product and strength of brand image
  (c) John Lewis: staff knowledge and customer service
  (d) Cadbury's chocolate: brand image

Chapter 2

1 Two from:
  (i) More potential customers
  (ii) Opportunity for economies of scale
  (iii) Can use mass media to advertise
2 Two from:
  (i) Can charge higher prices
  (ii) Higher profit margins
  (iii) Less expensive to enter
3 The PESTLE factors: political, economic, social, technological, legal, environmental
4 (i) Lower prices
  (ii) Better quality
  (iii) More innovation
5 Market research
6 Qualitative
7 Secondary
8 Primary
9 Quantitative
10 Product-orientated
11 (i) Small sample size
   (ii) Poorly selected sample
12 (i) Websites gathering information
   (ii) Social media gathering information
   (iii) Databases to help analyse data
13 (i) Products and services can be designed to suit specific customers
   (ii) Meeting customers' needs precisely allows a higher price to be charged
   (iii) Promotional activity is easier to target
14 Gaps in a market or the ideal positioning for a product
15 (i) Lowest cost
   (ii) Differentiation

16 (i) Aldi and Lidl have taken market share from Tesco.
   (ii) Aldi and Lidl have pushed value for money further up the agenda for many customers — encouraging Tesco to respond with price-match-type promotions.
   (ii) Aldi and Lidl have offered no-frills customer service, which has highlighted to Tesco the need to increase the quality of its customer service in order to stand out.
17 (a) iPhone: design and functions
   (b) Yorkie: chunkiest bar on the market
   (c) Nando's: trendiest among a certain age group
18 Efficiency is likely to mean lowest cost, meaning the firm can charge lower prices than anyone else and still make a profit
19 (i) Protects firms from the actions of competitors
   (ii) Allows prices to be raised without damaging demand very much
20 Successful advertising can increase consumers' perceived value of the product, often by attaching desirable images to the consumption of the product or service

Chapter 3

1 Seven from:
  (i) Price
  (ii) Changes in the prices of substitutes and complementary goods
  (iii) Changes in consumer incomes
  (iv) Fashions, tastes and preferences
  (v) Advertising and branding
  (vi) Demographics
  (vii) External shocks
  (viii) Seasonality
2 They are complementary, so demand for cars should rise
3 They are substitutes, so demand for Nikes should rise
4 (i) Arrival of a new competitor such as Costa
  (ii) Major local roadworks; new parking charges
5 If costs of production rise, firms will supply less and vice versa, because increased costs of production mean less profit can be made

6 As the robot is likely to cut the costs of production, supply would increase

7 A bad harvest caused by the weather

8 (i) To encourage the supply of green energy technologies

(ii) To create jobs

9 Supply would increase

10 Commodities

11 As price rises, fewer people are willing to buy

12 As price rises, firms are willing to supply more

13 Equilibrium

14 Two from:

(i) Changes in the prices of substitutes and complementary goods

(ii) Changes in consumer incomes

(iii) Fashions, tastes and preferences

(iv) Advertising and branding

(v) Demographics

(vi) External shocks

(vii) Seasonality

15 Two from:

(i) Change in costs of production

(ii) Introduction of new technology

(iii) Change in indirect taxes

(iv) Government subsidies

(v) External shocks

16 Inelastic

17 Decreased

18 (i) Product differentiation

(ii) Availability of substitutes

(iii) Branding and brand loyalty

19 (i) Sales forecasting

(ii) Deciding pricing strategy

20 Price elasticities change regularly, making it hard to use it to help predict the future

21 +1.5%

22 −2

23 (i) Who buys the product

(ii) Whether it is an indulgence or a necessity

24 (i) Income elasticity may have changed

(ii) The economic forecasts used to estimate a change in real incomes may be wrong

25 Inferior good

26 (a) Up

(b) Down

(c) Down

(d) Up

Chapter 4

1 (i) Aesthetics

(ii) Function

(iii) Economy of manufacture

2 Firms looking to use low cost as a point of competitive advantage

3 Three from:

(i) Adds value

(ii) Can reduce manufacturing costs

(iii) Can provide a point of differentiation

(iv) Improves brand image

(v) May boost brand loyalty

4 Three from:

(i) Sustainability

(ii) Reuse

(iii) Waste minimisation

(iv) Recycling

5 Designers should design with only ethically sourced ingredients/components in mind

6 (i) Seasonal price promotions

(ii) BOGOF

7 A problem with one product may affect all products carrying the corporate brand

8 Three from:

(i) Advertising

(ii) Sponsorship

(iii) Digital media

(iv) USP

9 Digital media has allowed the spread of 'word of mouth' to become far wider and much faster

10 Consumers will only pay a high price if the new product is unique, not a copy of an existing product

11 A low-priced launch may devalue its brand in the eyes of consumers

12 Unit cost

13 Low, or certainly no higher than their main rivals

14 With nothing to differentiate the product, pricing will need to be close to rivals

15 Unit cost = 4p + 3p + 1p + (£24/600) = 12p

Add 200% mark-up = 12p + 24p = 36p selling price per bun

16 If consumers cannot find a way to buy a product, sales targets will not be achievable

17 Producers sell to wholesalers who can then sell on to a wide range of retailers, allowing producers to get their product into many smaller retailers

18 (i) Benefit: complete control over how its product is sold

   (ii) Drawback: extra cost involved in running retail outlets

19 Small producers can now use direct channels of distribution that reach a very wide audience online via their own website or a platform such as eBay

20 (i) Introduction

   (ii) Growth

   (iii) Maturity

   (iv) Decline

21 Development

22 (i) Understanding the needs and wants of the market

   (ii) Creativity to solve problems

   (iii) Finding and committing the resources (money and people)

23 (i) Problem child

   (ii) Rising star

   (iii) Cash cow

   (iv) Dog

24 (i) Looks to the future

   (ii) Is achievable

   (iii) Is company-specific

25 Two from:

   (i) Offers control over promotion

   (ii) Gains wide distribution

   (iii) Can allow a firm to influence pricing in the market

26 Two from:

   (i) Allows a firm to charge higher prices

   (ii) Can meet consumer needs more closely

   (iii) May face less direct competition

27 While consumers make decisions based partly on emotion, business to business marketing relies simply on exactly what product can be delivered at the right price with the right level of reliability in terms of quality and timing

Chapter 5

1 Three from:

   (i) Multi-skilling

   (ii) Part-time and temporary working

   (iii) Flexible hours and home-working

   (iv) Outsourcing

   (v) Zero-hours contracts

2 Cash flow will be damaged in the short term as redundancy payments are made. In the long term, with lower costs, cash flow will improve

3 Collective bargaining

4 Two from:

   (i) Tailored to the company's own way of working

   (ii) No need to send staff out on expensive courses

   (iii) Instant advice can be given following an error

5 (i) A wider range of methods can be learned

   (ii) Fewer distractions than at the workplace

6 Interviewer bias or prejudice may affect the outcome

7 Two from:

   (i) Quicker and cheaper

   (ii) Promotion opportunities could motivate staff

   (iii) No need for induction training

   (iv) Better knowledge of applicants

8 Two from:

   (i) A wider pool of applicants

   (ii) Brings in new ideas

   (iii) Prevents creating a vacancy elsewhere in the business

9 Matrix

10 Flat structures have wide spans of control, forcing managers to allow subordinates to make their own decisions as they cannot closely supervise them all the time

11 Tall structures have many layers, offering plenty of scope to be moved up to the next level

12 All decision-making is kept at the very highest levels of the structure in a centralised organisation

13 (i) Scope to show initiative: Maslow self-actualisation or Herzberg meaningful and interesting work

   (ii) Extent of delegation: Maslow esteem or Herzberg's achievement

   (iii) Responsibility: Maslow esteem or Herzberg's responsibility

   (iv) Receiving all information required to perform a job: Herzberg spoke of the need for direct communication as part of job enrichment and saw company policy as a hygiene factor

   (v) Opportunities for promotion: Maslow's esteem needs and Herzberg's advancement

14 Taylor believed people worked to maximise their income. Therefore, people will work harder if working harder allows them to earn more money. Therefore, if a business wants an employee to work harder, they must ensure that the amount of work done is directly linked to the amount of pay the employee receives

15 This should mean that even if extra pay is earned, the firm will have more products available to sell in order to generate a higher revenue which can be used to cover higher wage costs

16 Money

17 Human relations

18 (i)   Physical

(ii) Safety

(iii) Social

(iv) Esteem

(v) Self-actualisation

19 (i)   Hygiene: company policy, supervision, pay, interpersonal relations, working conditions

(ii) Motivators: achievement, recognition, meaningful, interesting work, responsibility, advancement

20 Motivation means doing something because you want to do it, perhaps finding out more about Herzberg because you are fascinated by his theory, whereas movement is doing something to achieve a reward (perhaps your parents have offered you cash for grades) or to avoid a threat (will there be a phone call home of you don't hand in your homework?)

21 (i)   Piecework

(ii) Commission

(iii) Bonus

22 (i)   Job enrichment

(ii) Empowerment

(iii) Delegation

23 Team-working

24 Staff who are being handed decision-making power may lack the experience necessary to make the right decisions without prior training

25 (i)   Performance-related pay

(ii) Profit-sharing

(iii) Possibly bonuses

26 (a) Democratic (using management by objectives)

(b) Paternalistic

(c) Autocratic

(d) Laissez-faire

27 With few staff, the entrepreneur, who naturally is likely to be making key decisions on what the business should be doing and how to get around problems, will be unlikely to afford to hire a manager whose focus would be on the detailed implementation of the leader's plans and ideas. Instead, one person will have to perform two significantly different functions

Chapter 6

1 (i)   Noticing that a certain type of business does not exist in the local area

(ii) Spotting local behaviour that suggests a need exists for a certain type of service

2 Following the credit crunch, banks often see start-ups as particularly high-risk and low-return customers

3 (i)   Measuring performance objectively

(ii) Stepping back from the day-to-day challenges to think strategically

(iii) An eye for detail

(iv) Loving what they do

4 (i)   Profit maximising

(ii) Profit satisficing

5 Accepts risk as a fact of business life but only takes on sensible risks, where the rewards outweigh the risk

6 Three from:

(i)   Finance providers

(ii) Customers

(iii) Staff

(iv) Suppliers

7 Maximising profit may involve exploiting customers, destroying a business's reputation

8 Operating in an ethical way is likely to lead to extra costs

9 So the whole business is aiming to achieve the same thing

10 Specific, Measurable, Achievable, Realistic, Time-bound

11 (i)   Survival

(ii)   Profit maximisation

(iii) Sales maximisation

(iv) Market share

(v)   Cost efficiency

(vi) Employee welfare

(vii) Customer satisfaction

(viii) Social objectives

12 (i)   Sole trader

(ii) Partnership

13 £50,000

14 Two from:

(i)   Access to a tried and tested formula for business success

(ii) Support from the franchisor in providing materials and fixtures and fittings

(iii) Advice and training on all business functions

(iv) Possibility of a national advertising campaign from the franchisor

(v) A guaranteed local monopoly for that brand

(vi) Easier access to loans as banks recognise the lower risk involved in starting as a franchisee

15 Two from:
   (i) The franchisee may feel frustrated at being unable to make decisions dictated by the franchisor
   (ii) There is likely to be an initial franchise fee to buy the licence (perhaps several hundred thousand pounds for the most popular franchised brands)
   (iii) The franchisor will also expect royalties, a percentage of revenue

16 The value of the next best option forgone when a business decision is made

17 The process of compromise between conflicting objectives when making a decision

18 Not all profit is retained for use within the business and in the early stages of a business, there may not have been time to build up sufficient retained profit to finance growth

19 (i) Interest payments
   (ii) Repayments of the original sum borrowed

20 Many entrepreneurs are successful because they keep an eye on absolutely everything happening in the business and make all the decisions. Passing decision-making power to others is therefore very hard for many

Chapter 7

1 Many entrepreneurs fail to allocate enough of their start-up capital to working capital requirements, spending too much instead on fixed assets. In addition, entrepreneurs who overestimate revenue may run out of working capital, with not enough cash flowing back into the business

2 Budgets

3 Efficiency

Chapter 8

1 (i) Loans
   (ii) Overdrafts

2 Share capital

3 (i) Starting up
   (ii) Growing
   (iii) Dealing with a cash flow problem
   (iv) Financing extra materials needed when a large order is received

4 (i) Sole trader
   (ii) Partnership

5 Shareholders

6 Two from:
   (i) Peer-to-peer funding
   (ii) Crowdfunding
   (iii) Share capital

   (iv) Business angels
   (v) Venture capital

7 If a sole trader does not pay up, their own personal assets can be used to settle debts; this is not possible with a limited company

8 Finance providers

9 The cash flow forecast

10 Monthly balance or net cash flow

11 Usually by using an overdraft facility

Chapter 9

1 Three from:
   (i) HR
   (ii) Production
   (iii) Cash flow forecast
   (iv) Profit forecasts
   (v) Budgets

2 (i) Consumer trends
   (ii) Economic variables
   (iii) Actions of competitors

3 With more time to pass before the forecast becomes reality, there is more time for changes in the business environment to mess up the accuracy of the forecast by affecting sales

4 (i) Sales volume
   (ii) Sales value

5 Costs that do not change in relation to output

6 Costs that change in direct proportion to output

7 This helps to spread fixed costs over more units of output, reducing the fixed costs carried by each unit

8 Fixed costs / (selling price – variable cost per unit)

9 The vertical distance between revenue and total costs.

10 (i) Fixed costs
   (ii) Total costs
   (iii) Total revenue

11 Current output minus break-even output

12 The break-even would be lower

13 The break-even point would be higher

14 Three from:
   (i) To prevent over-spending
   (ii) To provide a yardstick against which to measure performance
   (iii) To allow spending power to be delegated
   (iv) To motivate staff in a department

15 (i) Historical budgeting
   (ii) Zero-based budgeting

16 Adverse

17 Favourable

Chapter 10

1 (i)   Gross profit
   (ii) Operating profit
   (iii) Profit for the year (net profit)

2 Profit is an absolute number – an amount of pounds – while profitability states profit as a percentage of sales revenue

3 Statement of comprehensive income (profit and loss account)

4 A product sold on credit generates revenue when it is sold, but no cash inflow until the customer pays at the end of the credit period

5 On a statement of financial position, otherwise known as a balance sheet

6 (a) (i) Current ratio
       (ii) Acid test ratio
   (b) (i) Current ratio should be 1.5:1
       (ii) Acid test should be around 1:1

7 Three from:
   (i)   Selling under-used fixed assets such as equipment or machinery
   (ii) Raising more share capital
   (iii) Increasing long-term borrowing through loans
   (iv) Postponing planned investments

8 Without managing working capital effectively the firm may run out of cash

9 Failure to understand customers (poor research) can lead to poor decisions within the marketing mix: unwanted product features, poor pricing decisions, etc. These are likely to mean sales are poor, so cash inflows dry up

10 If the business is unable to meet demand because it does not have sufficient stock, customers are likely eventually to go to rivals, leading to a fall in sales

11 Three from:
   (i)   Technological change
   (ii) Arrival of a new competitor
   (iii) Economic conditions
   (iv) The actions of banks

Chapter 11

1 Labour intensive

2 Efficiency includes consideration of wastage, not just speed

3 (i)   Age and quality of machinery
   (ii) Skills and experience of staff
   (iii) Level of employee motivation

4 $\dfrac{\text{output}}{\text{number of workers}}$

5 $\dfrac{\text{current output}}{\text{maximum possible output}} \times 100$

6 Fixed costs are spread over more units, therefore fixed cost per unit will be lower

7 (i)   No room to take on extra orders
   (ii) No time for maintenance or training

8 (i)   Increase sales volume
   (ii) Reduce maximum capacity

9 (a) Sales will be 1,000 units, so total contribution = 1,000 × £250 = £250,000. Deduct fixed costs to calculate profit: £250,000 – £120,000 = £130,000
   (b) Sales will be 600 units, so total contribution = 600 × £250 = £150,000. Deducting fixed costs gives a profit of: £150,000 – £120,000 = £30,000

10 Buffer stock (or minimum stock)

11 The horizontal gap between the re-order level and the delivery arriving shows the time taken to deliver; also known as lead time

12 Three from:
   (i)   Opportunity cost
   (ii) Cash flow problems
   (iii) Increased storage
   (iv) Increased financing costs
   (v)   Increased wastage

13 Two from:
   (i)   Lost customers
   (ii) Delays in production
   (iii) Lost reputation

14 With no buffer stock, production will halt if a delivery is delayed or contains faulty materials. This means the firm is highly dependent upon its suppliers delivering high-quality supplies with absolute reliability

15 If more is being produced, stock will be used more quickly, so the line representing the level of stock would fall more steeply if production levels increased

16 Quality inspectors

17 Cell

18 Quality circles

19 Production staff themselves

20 (i)   Allows a price premium to be charged: if price can be pushed up more than cost per unit, profit margins will rise
   (ii) Helps to gain distribution with retailers: gaining extra distribution helps to boost revenues
   (iii) Creates brand loyalty and repeat purchase: may save on advertising spending, reducing the cost of marketing
   (iv) Can help to build a brand reputation that spreads to other products: may allow

successful product launches, boosting revenues elsewhere in the portfolio, with relatively low product launch marketing costs

Chapter 12

1 Prices are rising more slowly
2 Consumers are likely to accept price increases without demand being damaged significantly
3 Spiced
4 Three from:
   (i) Demand falls as consumers' disposable incomes fall
   (ii) Consumers are less willing to borrow to buy
   (iii) Firms that owe money will face higher interest costs
   (iv) Investment is harder to justify as keeping the money in the bank is more attractive
5 Luxury goods (those with a positive income elasticity greater than 1)
6 (i) Increased costs
   (ii) Less wastage
7 The Health and Safety Executive
8 The employer
9 Two from:
   (i) Pricing
   (ii) Collusion
   (iii) Mergers
   (iv) Takeovers
10 Oligopoly
11 Two from:
   (i) Higher prices
   (ii) Less innovation
   (iii) Less choice
   (iv) Poorer service
12 Three from:
   (i) Branding
   (ii) Product features
   (iii) Product design
   (iv) Advertising
   (v) Technical innovations
13 A feature of a market that makes it hard for new entrants to successfully enter